open-ended logic

Why the best companies in the world are the best companies in the world.

KEVIN RAGSDALE

Prepared for publication by 40DayPublishing.com

Cover by Adam Ragsdale (AdamRagsdale.art)

Printed in the United States of America

Contents

For the best family in the world

Introduction

...The problem with logic is that it kills off magic.
Or, as Niels Bohr apparently once told Einstein, 'You are not thinking, you are merely being logical.'

Rory Sutherland, Alchemy

What if I told you that manned flight should have, on paper, been invented by someone other than the Wright brothers? In fact, all roads pointed to one man.

A brilliant mind, Samuel Langley was the inaugural director of the Allegheny Observatory, transforming a struggling institution into a beacon of achievement. He was behind the Allegheny Time System – a pioneering time standard that served Allegheny city businesses and the Pennsylvania Railroad. Add to that, his invention of the bolometer, crucial for measuring infrared radiation and a precursor to today's tools for assessing solar energy on earth. Oh, and his name is permanently stamped on the Langley Institute.

Starting off as an astronomer, Langley began dabbling in the mysteries of flight while teaching physics and astronomy at the Allegheny Observatory. By 1887, he penned *Experiments in Aerodynamics*, a work later embraced by the Smithsonian Institute in 1891.

His flight model? Launch a winged aircraft using a catapult, much like the mechanism of a rubber band. This method relied on the momentum generated by the catapult, propelling the aircraft into a glide. Featuring dual wings and a quad-winged rotor, this sleek wooden glider was perched on a houseboat style base located on the Chopawamsic Island's edge, overlooking the Potomac River.

Langley's credentials were impeccable. A series of successful tests, the pinnacle being a 300-yard glider flight, earned him significant funding. With a grant of $50,000 from the War Department and an additional $20,000 from the Smithsonian (a staggering $2.57 million today), he embarked on creating a manned aircraft. The War Department's faith in him was so profound that this grant was the highest-ever allocation for weapon development. Christened the "Aerodrome" – derived from Greek meaning "air runner" – Langley's vision seemed poised for historical recognition.

But then, two bicycle enthusiasts, sparked by tales of Langley's endeavors in 1896, entered the scene. While Langley basked in the spotlight, Wilbur and Orville Wright nursed a quiet, burgeoning dream: achieving flight.

That day.

The sand was soft and the shoreline steady, where outside temperatures hovered around the low forties at 10:35 a.m. on December 17, 1903. Brothers Orville and Wilbur Wright overlooked the beach of Kitty Hawk, North Carolina. Though they had been there many times before, this was quite different. Their arduous journey had led to this moment.

Three days earlier in his first flight, Wilbur crashed within three seconds of takeoff. Having repaired the aircraft, Orville now sat in the pilot seat and began the process of lift off. December 17 etched itself in history as Orville managed to make the first successful manned flight – 120 feet and a total of 12 seconds – before a soft crash landing. Repairs were made throughout the brisk day, and the brothers successfully flew four flights. During the last flight, their "flying machine" flew 852 feet with a total airtime of 59 seconds - five times longer than the first flight that day!

Changes in history come in the form of thoughts, distance, years, days, hours, and seconds. When vision is truly sought after and embedded in the hearts of individuals and their teams, the ability to change history becomes a living reality.

Although underfunded and lacking manpower, the Wright brothers believed that if they pursued their impossible dream of flight day-in and day-out, their vision would come to life. Their spurring passion essentially changed transportation and technological innovation. Focusing on their dream birthed their vision, and their vision was a catalyst that changed history.

Vision removes barriers and fosters unity. It gives us focus and a clear path – it gives us hope. With this foundation of hope, the vision becomes the narrator of our own stories as we create, imagine, and dream. Without a vision, space travel becomes impossible, a drawing of a mouse simply stays the drawing of a mouse, a search engine doesn't become a source of truth, or a fading heart doesn't find a replacement. Without a vision, people perish–we perish.

Nine days before the Wright brothers' success, on December 9, 1903, Samuel Pierpont Langley, very publicly – with fanfare, fireworks, and an extremely well-funded bank account – watched the last attempt of his flying machine disastrously launch and quickly topple into the Potomac. It begs the question, did Samuel Langley have the vision? If so, why would Langley's attempt largely fail in comparison to the Wright brothers? Maybe the better question to ask–did Langley possess the right vision? Or was this simply another accomplishment to add to his trophy collection? The Wright brothers pursued an invention that would alter the course of transportation. Their passion was broken down into the *how's* and *what's*. Their curiosity and persistence gave way to the *when* and *where*. And their vision became their *why*.[1]

The tale of the Wright brothers versus Langley is reminiscent of the biblical David and Goliath story. It is a testament to how a deeply rooted vision, accompanied by action, can transform ordinary into extraordinary. Within us all lies this capability - whether as individuals, teams, or entities.

Visions trickle up and down. The Wright brothers believed it, worked it, and sold the "what if" vision to their team. It grew into something great. And then, it flew.

Core. Structure. Culture.

"Innovate or die."

Peter Drucker

When you hear names like Apple, Starbucks, Disney, or Facebook, what conjures up in your mind? Many might envision giants that rose above the competition, not merely through superior products but a unique vision. But have you ever wondered how they reached those dizzying heights? Was it simply a logical, step-by-step process, or did they dare to dream beyond the horizon and chase a seemingly impossible vision?

The world of business often lauds the virtues of logic and reason, of predictable strategies and guaranteed results. But what if this isn't the only way? What if, instead of seeing logic as a linear path, we viewed it as something more open-ended?

Open-Ended Logic suggests that, in our rapidly evolving era of technology and innovation, the traditional paths labeled 'logical' might not always lead to the pinnacle of success. Instead, the key might lie in the uncharted territories of our imagination, in the audacious dreams we're often told are too risky or unrealistic.

While logic anchors our actions in reality, our imagination allows us to explore possibilities without bounds. Combined, they can lead to transformative ideas. Consider Apple's audacity to redefine personal technology or Starbucks' vision of a third place between work and home. Think of Disney's belief in creating unparalleled magical experiences or Facebook's goal to connect the world.

It's crucial not to misinterpret this as a call to abandon logic entirely, but rather to reconsider how we define it. It's about balancing the analytical with the imaginative, ensuring we don't close doors because tradition hasn't walked that path before.

As you delve deeper into this concept, challenge your perceptions. Let creativity guide your understanding of business. Remember, every groundbreaking invention, every global company, and every revolutionary idea began as a mere thought in someone's mind. Maybe it's time to let imagination and a new kind of logic co-pilot the journey to success.

Let's begin with the nitty-gritty.

Open-Ended Logic: Breaking the Mold of Conventional Thinking

When you hear "Open-Ended Logic" (OEL), it might sound contradictory at first. Logic is often synonymous with reason and being open-ended with endless possibilities. How can the two coexist? OEL challenges conventional thinking. It suggests that perhaps what we've deemed logical isn't the ceiling but merely a steppingstone to the stars of greater innovation.

The Illogic of Being Logical.

If logic is more or less rational, illogic should be irrational, right? When behavior goes against the norm, like when someone eats moldy food or intentionally cuts in line at your favorite Disneyland ride, illogical behavior is not an acceptable characteristic.

Imagine logic as being open-ended—essentially limitless in scope and possibility. It's not the curtailing of wild thoughts but rather the harnessing of imagination and innovation. Traditional logic can sometimes act as chains; OEL seeks to break them. This 'illogical' thinking has fueled many breakthroughs. Critics said the iPhone would fail because no one would pay $600 for a phone—that's just irrational! Others said Starbucks couldn't sell a $5 cup of coffee—that it's illogical because anyone can make a pitcher for less than fifty cents at home. But Apple and Starbucks, with their 'illogical' visions, transformed those criticisms into massive successes.

Consider the audacity of John F. Kennedy, who envisioned sending a man to the moon within a decade—a dream realized on June 20, 1969, when Apollo 11 landed, yes, on the moon, just shy of seven years after Kennedy's death on November 22, 1963. What an incredibly illogical and perhaps magical thought brought to life.[2] It was a seemingly illogical aspiration, yet it became a monumental achievement. This encapsulates the spirit of OEL—dreaming the 'impossible' and then making it happen.

Why Embrace OEL? In a rapidly evolving world, if organizations aren't constantly questioning, innovating, and challenging norms, they risk becoming obsolete. OEL acts as a catalyst for innovation, pushing entities to not just succeed, but to redefine success. It is built on three pivotal segments: core, structure, and culture. Like the three parts of a bicycle wheel, these segments drive forward momentum, ensuring that businesses remain dynamic, relevant, and impactful.

The Future of Organizational Thinking

Open-Ended Logic is not just a novel concept—it's a necessary one. As Bob Iger aptly said, "Progress waits for no one." OEL serves as a guide to unlock superior products, exceptional service, and, most importantly, the immense potential of human resources. Embrace it and let your business soar to unprecedented heights.[3]

The Wheel of Open-Ended Logic

The OEL Core Is Equivalent to the Hub of a Wheel.

VISION: **Where** we want to go + **Why** we're going there = our Purpose

MISSION: **What** we're going to do and **How** we're going to get there

VALUES: **Who** we are and want to be

The Three Sections of OEL:

1. CORE (HUB)
2. STRUCTURE (SPOKES)
3. CULTURE (RIM)

Shared Roots of Greatness: The DNA of Success

In *Great by Choice*, Jim Collins underscores a compelling idea: the core essence that molds great leaders is often universal. This premise isn't limited to individuals; it's also mirrored in successful organizations. Though industries and businesses may vary, the DNA of successful entities shares common threads.[4]

Introducing Open-Ended Logic (OEL), a concept that dovetails seamlessly with Collins' observations. While many businesses strategize around mitigating risks and managing unfavorable outcomes, OEL prompts a paradigm shift. Instead of merely managing expectations, it emphasizes unlocking potential, harnessing capabilities, and consistently delivering outstanding results. It's about nurturing an environment where innovation isn't an outlier but a standard procedure; where success isn't a fluke, but a reproducible outcome.

But for OEL to truly thrive, there needs to be cohesion in vision across the organization. A vision misaligned with the collective effort of its workforce remains an intangible dream. Just as the DNA of an organism instructs its growth, the shared values, principles, and mission within an organization guide its trajectory. In essence, without unity in purpose, vision lacks legs.

In a world where the business landscape is constantly shifting, and where innovation and adaptability are prized commodities, OEL offers a compass. It's not about changing with the times, but rather setting the pace for the times to follow. And at the heart of it all is a collective vision, bound by shared values and a laser focused mission, driving success not as an exception but as a rule.

Crafting the DNA of Business Excellence: A Deep Dive into Open-Ended Logic (OEL)

At the heart of any successful organization lies a guiding force, an ethos, which many term as the Vision, Mission, and Values (VMV). This book aims to shed light on the transformative power of VMV, exploring its central role in the concept of Open-Ended Logic (OEL).

The potency of VMV within the OEL framework cannot be overstated. It is the bedrock, the very essence of the organizational DNA. It's not enough for these foundational principles to merely exist; their clarity, relevance, and embodiment are paramount. Without a crystal clear VMV, an organization's journey lacks direction and purpose.

But VMV is just the inception. Structure builds on this core. Just as the skeletal system provides shape and support to the body, organizational structure strengthens and guides the corporate entity. It elevates teams from mediocrity to excellence, transforming good companies into industry titans. Structure ensures that the grand vision isn't just a lofty idea but is rooted in actionable strategies and processes.

With a robust VMV and a lucid structure in place, the evolution of an organization's culture naturally follows. It flourishes, becoming a living testament to the company's ideals. Culture isn't just about team outings or corporate events; it's the palpable energy, the shared ethos, and the collective ambition that propels an organization forward.

Together, the triad of Core (VMV), structure, and culture are the keystones of the OEL framework. Yet, a mere acknowledgment of these principles isn't sufficient. VMV isn't a decorative statement to be displayed on a company website. It isn't a memo to be circulated or a speech to be delivered. It is the lifeblood of an organization. It should be evident in every meeting, every project, every decision, and every interaction inside and outside the organization, to the point of being felt without words. True success lies in making VMV and OEL not just a corporate strategy but an ingrained way of life—a heartbeat that resonates across every tier of the organization.

Xerox's Lost Vision: An Emblematic Tale of Missed Potential

In wrapping up this introduction, let's reflect on an iconic misstep in business history: the Xerox conundrum. Xerox PARC, established in 1970, stood at the forefront of technological innovation. Their groundbreaking work in graphics computing, particularly the development of the first conceived "mouse", had the potential to revolutionize personal computing.

However, what Xerox lacked wasn't innovation; it was vision. They failed to recognize and harness the transformative potential of what they had created. Their oversight became another company's windfall. In 1979, a curious Steve Jobs from the then-up-and-coming Apple was granted access to Xerox's cutting-edge innovations. He didn't just see a mouse or a graphical user interface; he saw the future.[5]

The rest, as they say, is history. Apple took these foundational technologies and redefined personal computing with the introduction of the Macintosh. Xerox, on the other hand, was left to ponder what could have been. Their lapse underscores the criticality of not just innovating, but understanding the broader implications of that innovation.

Open-Ended Logic (OEL) encapsulates this very principle. It encourages businesses to blend logic with creative foresight, to seek the extraordinary within the ordinary. Instead of mere innovation, OEL champions vision-driven innovation. It's not just about creating; it's about understanding the broader potential of that creation and acting on it. Xerox's story serves as a poignant reminder of the immense value of this philosophy. For in the realm of business, vision isn't just clarity of sight; it's the ability to dream, to foresee, and to act decisively.

PART 1:
CORE / THE HUB

VISION

MISSION

VALUES

Vision

Where there is no vision, the people perish.

Proverbs 29:18

Dictionary.com defines VISION as "to envision, or picture mentally." *Verb*

The Spectrum of Vision: From Dreams to Reality

Vision is akin to foresight, a deep-rooted ability to visualize what lies ahead. It's looking at a rundown home and seeing a masterpiece awaiting transformation. It's imagining intricate details of an app before it even exists, or visualizing humans setting foot on Mars and thinking, *"Yeah, we can do that!"* At its core, vision is about perception, the ability to discern possibilities beyond the obvious.

Like a mosaic gradually taking shape, visions aren't typically sudden revelations. Instead, they unfurl over time, evolving from humble beginnings to magnificent crescendos. The annals of history are replete with tales of visions—some that catapulted to unprecedented heights, and others that nosedived into obscurity. These stories prod us to question: Why do certain visions ascend to glory while others wither away? What differentiates a successful vision from an unsuccessful one?

Exploring the Genesis of Vision:

The Source: Where do visions emanate from? Are they the products of rigorous brainstorming sessions, spontaneous epiphanies, or perhaps a merger of both?

Transmission: How are visions communicated across an organization? Is it enough to merely articulate them, or should they be woven into the fabric of the company, ensuring everyone—right from the top brass to the newest recruit—grasps, nurtures, and propels it?

In this section, we'll embark on a journey exploring the gamut of visions. From audacious endeavors that defied all odds to those that lost their way but found a beacon in time, and to visions that, unfortunately, dwindled into the abyss. Through these tales, we'll distill the essence of what makes a vision truly transformative and how it can be harnessed to steer organizations toward unparalleled success.

Bob Noyce: The Visionary Behind Modern Technology

In the early days of aviation, as the world marveled at the possibility of humans taking to the skies, a young boy named Bob (Robert Noyce), harbored his own dream. A dream not just to fly, but to innovate and break barriers.

Growing up in the heartland of America, Bob's imagination knew no bounds. His childhood aspirations came to life when, with a paltry sum of $4.35, he constructed a rudimentary glider. Made out of pine and cheese cloth, this ambitious project saw fruition in his own backyard. With the assistance of his older brother, the barn's roof served as the launchpad. The flight might have been short-lived, a mere 14 feet, but for Bob, it was a triumphant leap—a testament to human will and creativity.

The skies weren't the only frontier Bob intended to conquer. While flight remained a secondary passion, his true calling lay elsewhere. Guided by a relentless curiosity and a visionary spark, Bob ventured into the realm of electronics. He went on to co-invent something that would not just make headlines, but fundamentally reshape the world: the integrated circuit.[6]

The integrated circuit, a cornerstone of modern technology, has since become ubiquitous — powering everything from our wristwatches to supercomputers. This invention heralded the dawn of the digital age, and Bob, often dubbed the "Mayor of Silicon Valley," was at the heart of this revolution.

In reflecting upon Bob's journey, it's evident that it wasn't just his inventions that were groundbreaking; it was his incessant belief in the impossible. Whether launching a makeshift glider or pioneering electronic marvels, Bob Noyce embodied the spirit of a true visionary—someone who saw potential where others saw limits.

Shockley: The Genesis of Silicon Valley

In 1948, Bob Noyce received an offer he couldn't refuse. A direct call from none other than the Nobel Prize laureate, William Shockley. This wasn't just any job offer; it was an invitation to be a part of Shockley Semiconductor, the cutting-edge hub for electronic innovation. The transistor, originally conceived by Julius Lilienfeld in 1926, saw its practical evolution in 1947 under the watchful eyes of physicists John Bardeen, Walter Brattain, and William Shockley. Together at Bell Laboratories, they not only refined the transistor but initiated a technological revolution that birthed devices ranging from transistor radios to computers.

Shockley's brilliance was undeniable. Having etched his name alongside luminaries like Thomas Edison, he decided to carve a niche of his own. Assembling a team of eminent scientists, Shockley established his namesake company, Shockley Semiconductor, in what was then a nondescript part of Mountain View, California. This region, once characterized by sprawling vineyards, would soon morph into Silicon Valley, the world's epicenter for technological ingenuity and affluence.

Visions of companies often start as fleeting ideas. As they evolve and take form, they often find their way onto walls, entrance plaques, training manuals, and promotional materials. But a vision's true worth is measured not by its visibility but by its permeation into the company's culture. A vision should resonate, echo in every conversation, and reflect in every action. If it remains just a printed statement, it risks sinking into obscurity.

What's vital is that the vision connects with the essence, reason, and emotions of its team. Delving deeper into Noyce's narrative, which we'll elaborate on in later chapters, provides a blueprint of what a vision can and should achieve. It's paramount that the workforce, like the semiconductor team at Shockley's, feel an intrinsic connection to the foundational moments and beliefs of their institution. They should sense the same fervor and anticipation that pioneers like Noyce and Shockley felt, standing on the precipice of monumental change, fueled by a shared belief in their vision's transformative power. Only then does a vision truly breathe, evolve, and endure.

The Anatomy of Vision

Every vision, regardless of its scale or domain, is fueled by an inherent drive. From corporate visions to product-centric ones, the underlying principles that drive their success are remarkably consistent.

At the heart of any vision lies its core essence, and its success depends on how deeply it resonates with all stakeholders. Think of a vision as a seed. Simply throwing it onto the soil and hoping for it to grow isn't enough. It demands care, nurturing, and patience. The seed has to be sown rightly, watered regularly, and shielded against adversities. Similarly, merely articulating a vision won't suffice. It needs consistent reinforcement, care, and dedication to thrive.

For a vision to truly come alive, it has to be embedded in the daily lexicon of an organization. A successful vision statement isn't just profound; it's also concise, memorable, and easy to grasp. It should act as a unifying force, aligning everyone—whether they're in the C-suite or on the frontlines—toward a common purpose.

But how do you determine the essence of that vision? How do you mold it into a statement that inspires and drives action?

The journey to crystallizing a vision necessitates introspection and curiosity. It demands answers to the fundamental questions that drive Open-Ended Logic: Who are we? What do we aspire to be? When and where do we see ourselves achieving it? How will we traverse this journey? And, most importantly, why is this our chosen path?

The beauty of vision is its boundless potential. With the right nurture, commitment, and understanding, it can metamorphose from an abstract idea into a tangible reality, guiding us to destinations previously deemed unreachable.

Finding the vision that we all seek to attain and making it reality requires answering questions in our open-ended arsenal.

What?

What is the vision?

What does this vision accomplish?

Who?

Who needs to be involved to get the vision from concept to reality?

Who is/are the vision's beneficiary/beneficiaries?

Where?

Where do we begin the process of getting the vision started?

Where do we go to get the momentum to build the vision?

When?

When will the vision be ready to launch?

When will we know the vision has been accepted?

How?

How do we imbed the vision into the day-to-day working environment?

How will we know when we've achieved the vision?

Why?

Why is this vision important?

Why will people join in creating and executing the vision?

Vision Realized: Snow White's Legendary Tale

Although the Great Depression overshadowed the American economy in the late 1920s and early 1930s, a beacon of hope emerged from Walt Disney Productions. The popularity of "Mickey Mouse Silly Symphonies," short films designed to prelude main feature films, had brought Disney to the forefront. Yet, the prosperity that these shorts fetched was dwarfed by the revenues main feature films accrued for other studios. It became increasingly evident to Disney that their key to achieving revenues similar with bigger studios was in creating a full-length animation feature.

Interestingly, the concept wasn't entirely novel. A decade before *Snow White* graced the screen, Lotte Reiniger's *The Adventures of Prince*

Achmed, a 65-minute feature, employing the silhouette animation technique, had premiered in 1926. Though poorly performing at the box office, it was a technological marvel that hinted at the enormous potential of animation features.[7]

With *Snow White and the Seven Dwarfs*, Disney envisioned an animated extravaganza that would captivate audiences not just with its visuals, but with its heartwarming storyline depth. This ambitious undertaking demanded tremendous resources – a bigger team of artists, state-of-the-art infrastructure, and substantial capital investment. The sheer volume of labor required was astounding. For instance, even a fleeting moment on screen necessitated multiple drawings, with only a fraction making the final cut. The process was equally grueling for the film's musical compositions, with a majority ending up on the cutting room floor.

A typical short film, at this time, would have taken a substantial number of artists and hours to complete. For instance, each split second of the film would take twelve drawings for each character in a single scene. When a scene possessed several characters, one split second would have required fifty drawings or more. Every hundred drawings may have only produced ten drawings acceptable to use. Out of the artwork, the narrative within the story was executed.

Storyline crafting had always been Walt's forte. His success with "Mickey Mouse Silly Symphonies" had amplified his ability to fire up the imaginations of audiences. Yet, for his ambitious Snow White project, Walt recognized that exciting his internal team was paramount. These artists, animators, and musicians were the pillars on which his vision would be constructed.

Convincing them was crucial. Without their buy-in, Snow White would remain confined to sketches and storyboards. Walt believed that rallying his team around his vision was the first step. He knew he had to paint for them the picture of what *Snow White and the Seven Dwarfs* could be—a masterpiece etched in cinematic history.

After weeks of personally envisioning the storyline and bouncing ideas off close confidantes, like his wife Lillian and his trusted partner, Roy

Disney, Walt strategized the best approach to pitch the story to his artists. He knew that to make this vision soar from the drawing boards to the silver screen, he had to ensure that each artist felt deeply connected and indispensable to the journey of Snow White.

"I have a story to tell you."

In *How to Be Like Walt*, Pat Williams and Jim Denney describe how it went down on the night Walt sold *Snow White and the Seven Dwarfs* to his artists:

> *Within days, Walt gathered forty of his top animators. Opening his wallet, he handed each man some cash, then said, "I want you fellas to go have dinner and relax a little. Then come back to the studio.* ***I have a story to tell you****."*
>
> *The animators walked out of the studio, buzzing among themselves. After dinner, they gathered on a recording stage where Walt had set up folding chairs in a semicircle. The room was dark, like a movie theater, except at the front.*
>
> *There stood Walt, under a single light bulb, bouncing on his heels, a secretive smile on his face. Once everyone was present, Walt began to tell the story of 'Snow White and the Seven Dwarfs.'*
>
> *Walt didn't merely tell the story. He performed it, acting out every part. He became every character. His eyebrows arched, and his features twisted into those of the evil Queen. He tilted his face toward the bare light bulb, and its soft glow transformed his face into that of Snow White. Each character had a distinct voice and personality.*
>
> *Reaching the end of the tale, Walt paused—then said, "That is going to be our first feature-length animated film." If Walt had said those words at the beginning of his presentation, his artists would have thought he was crazy. Everyone knew there was no audience for an all-animated feature.*

> *But after watching Walt act out the story before their eyes, they believed it was not only possible, but practically an accomplished fact! Walt had the whole picture in his head—all they had to do was animate it.*
>
> *"Walt's greatest talent was his ability to get people fired up," said Disney historian Robert W. Butler. "The greatest show Walt ever put on was when he acted out the story of Snow White for his animators. They were so energized and inspired by his performance that it kept them going for the next four years."*

In the four years after Walt unveiled his vision, Walt Disney Productions faced the brink of failure, grappling with financial setbacks and Walt's own personal challenges. Within this tumultuous period, innovation thrived: groundbreaking technologies emerged, proficient artists elevated to mastery, and the dream was ultimately realized when *Snow White and the Seven Dwarfs* made its debut in Hollywood on December 21, 1937. The world welcomed it with open arms on February 4, 1938. As this masterpiece was taking flight, Walt's mind was in the infancy of shaping another dream: Disneyland.[8]

The Power Behind a Vision Statement

The journey from conceptualizing a vision to its tangible realization, especially with hopes of organic growth, holds a low chance of coming to fruition unless clarity is at the epicenter. Regardless of whether it concerns a business, a division, a product, or a service, a consistent and compelling vision is crucial.

Vision, Mission, Values Defined

Vision –

The act or power of imagination. (Merriam-Webster)

A vivid, imaginative conception or anticipation. (DICTIONARY.com)

Mission –

A specific task with which a person or a group is charged. (Merriam-Webster)

The business with which such a group is charged. Any important task or duty assigned, allotted, or self-imposed. Of or relating to a mission. (Dictionary.com)

Values –

Something, such as principle or quality, intrinsically valuable or desirable. (Merriam-Webster)

Ethics. Any object or quality desirable as a means or as an end in itself. (Dictionary.com)

Statement –

The act or process of stating or presenting orally or on paper. (Merriam-Webster)

A communication or declaration in speech or writing, setting forth facts, particulars, etc. (Dictionary.com)

We'll delve into how these three core components harmoniously interact to forge a company's foundational strength. Additionally, we'll examine various corporate pillars, explore the "who, what, when, where, how, and why" behind their triumphs and setbacks, and investigate their influence on outcomes for both staff and clientele.

Imagination to Imagineering

Disneyland (1954)

Walt's discussions about Disneyland began alongside his brother, Roy Disney, just as their animation venture began to gain momentum after fluctuating financial challenges. While Walt was passionate about transforming his amusement park idea into reality, he faced numerous obstacles. These hurdles included skeptical banks and, importantly, resistance from Roy, who was focused on their existing ventures and wary of allocating Disney funds to an endeavor outside their established business model. Despite the trepidation around investing profits into "another one of Walt's screwy ideas," Walt was resolute; for him, the vision of Disneyland was already set in motion.[9]

Walt's commitment to his dream led him to survey various amusement parks in the U.S. and Europe, searching for the perfect inspiration. He found it in Denmark's Tivoli Gardens. Celebrated as the second-oldest operating amusement park in the world, Tivoli's cleanliness and friendly ambiance captivated Walt. Armed with this inspiration and his signature Disney flair, Walt identified a suitable piece of land in Anaheim, California.[10]

Spurred by determination and passion, Walt founded Walter Elias Disney Enterprises (WED) in March of 1953. WED was "The only think tank created by Walt himself."[11] This was to lay the groundwork for Disneyland's design and technological elements. Assembling a team of engineers, artists, and designers, he termed these innovators 'Imagineers'. WED, being Walt's very own creation, symbolized his dedication to Disneyland. It soon became evident to others, including Roy, that Disneyland was an inevitability, especially given Walt's immovable commitment. Construction began on July 16, 1954, with just one year earmarked for completion.

In "How to Be Like Walt," Art Linkletter, a friend of Walt's, recounts a moment in 1954 when Walt, standing on the barren Anaheim plot, vividly described the entirety of Disneyland – from the intricacies of each ride to the strategic layout of his "wheel and spoke" design, ensuring visitors never felt fatigued or disoriented. From the Castle to Tomorrowland to the Firehouse, Walt's descriptions transformed the empty land into a vivid tapestry of attractions, rides, and experiences. For Walt, his vision was more than just a dream; it was a tangible future.

Walt's unyielding dedication, from mortgaging his own home to selling personal assets, fueled the energy and momentum required to make Disneyland a reality. And on July 17, 1955, that reality was shared with the world.

Visions become reality when organizations and teams:

- Commit
- Strategically plan
- Be bold
- Stay positive
- Exude confidence
- Illustrate through stories
- Take action

Rebounding After Visions Get Fuzzy

Walt Disney's passing on December 15, 1966, sent ripples of sorrow across the globe. Yet, the depth of this grief loomed over Disney headquarters. In the wake of the announcement, executives were moments away from shuttering Disneyland for the day as a mark of respect. However, a call from Lillian, Walt's wife, changed the course.

Relaying her message to Card Walker, the soon-to-be president, she expressed Walt's likely wish: to keep the park operational. This sentiment suggested Walt's vision would remain steadfast.[12]

In the subsequent years, notably until 1973, Walt Disney Productions realized another of Walt's grand designs by opening Walt Disney World in Orlando. While the entity continued to churn out family-centric content and amplified its theme parks, one couldn't help but wonder: was the underpinning vision still resonant?

With Walt Disney World's inauguration—a project exceeding $400 million—the company marked another accomplishment. Yet, a creeping descent began, characterized by a lack of clear direction. The torchbearers attempted to uphold Walt's blueprint, but it appeared increasingly nebulous and antiquated. Over time, this vision, once revolutionary, became lethargic and mediocre.

Tangible: Clear and definite; something that can be physically touched or felt.

Intangible: Elusive and abstract; beyond physical touch or simple understanding.

The challenge in following a vision of the past, whether that of Walt Disney - unequivocally one of the greatest visionaries of the twentieth century - or any other individual, is that the vision must consistently be reviewed and updated to remain futuristically relevant. In this case, Walt Disney's approach was slowly becoming irrelevant and passé. For an eighteen-year stint, the company held true to the past and the nostalgic feel of the theme parks. Yet, during this time, the company became increasingly insignificant, until 1984, when Michael Eisner was brought on as CEO and Frank Wells as President and COO to create and build the new vision. Eisner had the imagination and forethought to bring intangible ideas and dreams back to the Disney canvas, with the vision of making those ideas and dreams more tangible.

The purpose of the intangible is to make the tangible. Organizations that live in only a tangible world will deliver tangible energy - tangible results. In contrast, those who venture into the intangible often see their lofty visions materialize.

FedEx's Journey: From Rapid Deliveries to ZapMail's Misstep

FedEx built its reputation on swift mail delivery. The brainchild behind this innovative venture was Fredrick W. Smith, who had initially outlined this idea as a college assignment aimed at next-day mail delivery. Despite skepticism from his professor, Smith was determined to make his vision a reality. Through persistence and innovation, he transformed FedEx into a $50 billion revenue juggernaut, elevating his personal worth to $4 billion in the process. In a poetic twist, Smith later employed the very professor who doubted him, prominently displaying the original business plan under a glass dome at FedEx's headquarters.[13]

As FedEx flourished, Smith continued to seek expansion opportunities. The emergence of fax technology in 1983 presented another avenue. Smith envisioned an auxiliary FedEx service to rival these machines. By June 1984, this idea materialized as 'ZapMail'. However, within just two years, ZapMail devolved into a $317-million setback, despite enlisting a 1,300-strong workforce.

Smith's intent was clear: to rival fax machines and similar offerings. Yet, as Jonathan Coopersmith highlighted in his analysis for Texas A&M:

> *The fundamental flaw of ZapMail was the emphasis on centralized mailroom to mailroom delivery at a time when the trend was towards decentralized desktop to desktop delivery. Compounding this error was the equipment's incompatibility with any other fax system, barring ZapMail from the rest of the fax community.*

Visions blur when the benchmark is based on current or, worse, past standards and platforms. What is not entirely earthshaking is that when Smith announced that ZapMail was closing its doors, investors welcomed the news and the price per share surged 13 percent. It's bad enough when the vision is fuzzy for those within the corporation, but it's immensely worse when customers don't understand. When the vision unravels and confusion begins to corrupt relevance, it creates uncertainty in team members, customers, and stockholders.[14]

Eight Types of Vision Statements

- Short Vision Statements
- Quantitative Vision Statements
- Qualitative Vision Statements
- Competitor-Based Vision Statements
- Role Model Vision Statements
- Internal Transformation Vision Statements
- Detailed Vision Statements
- People Vision Statements

The Evolution of Vision and Navigating Hasty Choices

Vision statements, diverse in style and substance, range from concise one-liners to more detailed, evocative declarations that rally everyone towards a common goal. Forgoing a vision statement or hastily crafting one can be likened to boarding a flight without any knowledge of its destination.

Here, we'll explore various types of vision statements employed by companies in their journey toward growth and innovation. As we delve into these statements, it's intriguing to note that some of these companies, once market leaders, have lost their dominance over time. This decline can be attributed to shifting trends or, in certain instances, a drift away from their original vision.

Short Vision Statements

- LinkedIn – Create economic opportunities for every member of the global workforce.
- Under Armour – Empower Athletes Everywhere
- IKEA – To create a better everyday life for many people.

Quantitative Vision Statements

- Microsoft – A computer on every desk and in every home; all running Microsoft.
- Nike – Current: To be the number one athletic company in the world. ("Just do it", and they did!)
- For The Children (formerly Royal Family KIDS Camp) – Every foster child, ages 6-12, experiences a life-changing camp and mentoring club.

Qualitative Vision Statements

- Ford – To become the world's leading Consumer Company for automotive products and services.
- Southwest – The be the world's most loved, most efficient, and most profitable airline.
- Avon – To be the company that best understands and satisfies the product, service, and self-fulfillment needs of women—globally.

Competitor-Based Vision Statements

- Honda – in 1970: WE will destroy Yamaha.
- Nike – in the 1960s: Crush Adidas.

Role Model Vision Statements – using another company as an example

- Giro Sport Design – To become the Nike of the cycling industry.
- Stanford University – To become the Harvard of the West.
- Reach for Success – To become the next Tony Robbins in self-development.

Internal Transformation Vision Statements

- Sony – Become the company most known for changing the worldwide poor-quality image of Japanese products.
- U.S. Army – To transform ourselves into a new, leaner Army positioned for the 21st Century.

Detailed Vision Statements

Coca-Cola – "To achieve sustainable growth, we have established a vision with clear goals:

- Profit: Maximizing return to share owners while being mindful of our overall responsibilities.
- People: Being a great place to work where people are inspired to be the best they can be.
- Portfolio: Bringing to the world a portfolio of beverage brands that anticipate and satisfy people's desires and needs.
- Partners: Nurturing a winning network of partners and building mutual loyalty.
- Planet: Being a responsible global citizen that makes a difference.

Heinz – Our vision, quite simply, is to be: "The World's Premier Food Company, offering Nutritious, Superior Tasting Foods to People Everywhere."

Being the premier food company does not mean being the biggest, but it does mean being the best in terms of consumer value, customer service, team member talent, and consistent and predictable growth.[15]

Micro Visions Embedded Into Vision Statements

- People Vision
- Team Vision
- Product/Service Vision
- Business Vision
- Customer Vision

Vision incorporates everything from our people and customers to our businesses when defining the whole picture.

- **People** – Growth and acceleration. How do we grow as people and, with that growth, grow our organization?
- **Team** – What does our team look like in terms of characteristics, achievements, and values?
- **Product/Service** - What can we produce for the future that will meet the demands and needs of our customers.
- **Business** – How do we jump the short-term profit hurdles while our focus is on our long-term profitable growth?
- **Customer** – Who is our customer? How do we continue to show our value to our customers through our service and products?

The Vision Statement

- Who are we?
- What do we do?
- What do we want to do?
- Where do we want to go?
- Why do we exist?
- What do we want to become?

The culmination of the answers to these questions becomes the vision statement. The more thought and energy poured into defining the vision, the more definitive the vision statement.

Vision Indoctrination

One might wonder, how can we ensure that everyone actively partakes in and truly embodies the vision? The answer lies in simplicity. Startlingly, statistics reveal that 90 percent of team members aren't familiar with their company's vision statement. Furthermore, a mere 14 percent of companies believe their team members have a "good understanding" of the organization's direction and strategy. Such disconnection is not only surprising but also poses a significant challenge for organizations.[16]

Sustaining a Vision: Navigating the Journey to the Destination

Sometimes, our focus is solely on the destination, without much regard for the plane we're on, its cost, or the service we receive. Yet, the journey determines the destination. In the realm of business, it's essential to understand our desired endpoint, recognize who will guide us there, and chart the path forward. This embodies our destination, our team, our envisioned future, and the overarching vision.

The disconnect team members often feel from their company's vision, mission, and values can be traced back to leadership. The onus is on leaders to weave these perspectives into everyday interactions. Continuous onboarding and refresher training ensures team members recognize their role and, even more crucially, their place in the broader vision. When every team member truly grasps the vision, an organic momentum builds, propelling the organization towards its goals. They can only offer the necessary commitment when they have a personal connection and know they are part of the fabric that helps achieve the vision.

But is a vision merely a distant mirage we never truly reach? No matter which airline we choose, if we're unaware of our destination or the reasons propelling us there, trivial perks like peanuts and pretzels become irrelevant. The same principle applies to the vision and its combining elements. We should always aim for the intangible, knowing that a lack of vision can lead to our demise. Here, "perish" doesn't signify a literal end, but rather the waning commitment of our teams and organization. This firm commitment is the linchpin we desire in every individual and collectively as a team. When a united group of committed individuals strives collectively towards a shared vision, even the seemingly impossible becomes attainable.

Commitment: *the state or quality of being dedicated to a cause, activity, etc.*[17]

Are you and your organization dedicating the necessary time and effort to pave a clear path for individuals to truly commit? Organizations that embrace Open-Ended Logic don't merely take a gamble, hoping a brief introduction to their vision, mission, and values during an orientation will yield optimal outcomes.

The adage "slow is smooth and smooth is fast," borrowed from the Navy SEALs, encourages the importance of deliberate, careful actions leading to faster overall success. Similarly, in the realms of vision, mission, and values, clarity within an organization culminates in a profound appreciation and a more comprehensive grasp of the collective purpose we should all be seeking.

Mud Runs: Pushing Limits and Building Community

Historically, obstacle courses have been confined to P.E. classes and intense military training. Most of us might have glimpsed them only in war films. However, the 2009 debut of the show "American Ninja Warrior," inspired by Japan's "Sasuke," showcased daunting obstacle courses, and by summer 2017, had millions riveted.

In the last decade, entrepreneurs tapped into the rising enthusiasm for obstacle courses, turning them into public events across the globe. These events, known as mud runs, include popular names like Warrior Dash, Zombie, Gladiator Rock 'N Run, Battlefrog, Spartan Race, and Tough Mudder, with the latter two leading the pack.[18]

From the mountainous terrains of Pennsylvania, the shores of California, to the red mud expanses of Oklahoma, these obstacle courses have drawn participants. They call themselves, "Mud Runners," and they're not just the physically elite. Many are individuals seeking a weekend challenge without committing to professional sports or military service.

It might sound perplexing: why would anyone pay to test their physical limits, enduring bruises, and cuts? When Will Dean, the founder of Tough Mudder, pitched the idea, many were skeptical. Dean's response was insightful: "Most people who enter a race, a marathon, a triathlon—they aren't really racing, they are trying to do something for themselves."

Drawing from his military background, Dean understood the profound satisfaction and motivation derived from overcoming obstacles. His experience as a former counterterrorism officer only amplified this perspective. Thousands now participate in each event, with hundreds volunteering, embodying a tribal spirit. Dean's formula brings together diverse individuals, uniting them in their pursuit of completing the arduous 12-mile course.

The idea of paying money for a 12-mile obstacle course might seem far-fetched unless witnessed firsthand. But the dedication doesn't stop at the participants. The volunteers, integral to Tough Mudder's success, invest hours mapping, constructing, and test-running the courses. For them, it's not about monetary gain or fame; it's about being part of a grander mission and seeing it to fruition. Tough Mudder has evolved into a multi-million-dollar enterprise, demonstrating that its value extends well beyond mere financial gains.

For The Children (formerly Royal Family KIDS)

Vision: Every foster child, ages 6-12, experiences a life-changing camp and mentoring club.

Mission: Creating positive, life-changing moments for innocent children who have been victims of neglect, abuse, and abandonment.

Values: Treat People Royally, Keep Moving Forward, and Make Moments Matter.[19]

In 1985, Wayne and Diane Tesch founded Royal Family KIDS Camp, which has since updated its name to For The Children. They had the vision of a camp that would provide hope to foster children. The camp was to show God's love and support to kids, ages 6 to 12, who, not by their own doing, were subject to unthinkable tragedy, neglect, and abuse. Wayne and Diane simply wanted to do what they could to help kids in need. What started with a small vision for a camp in the mountains of Costa Mesa, California, has grown into a global outreach with kids' camps reaching around the world.

Who makes up the workforce of a For The Children camp? Volunteers. Why would volunteers participate in such a vision? To see "every foster child, ages 6-12, experience a life-changing camp..." For The Children camps are run primarily by volunteers who have caught Wayne and Diane's vision. They are lawyers, educators, culinary artists, medical professionals, artists, and even the younger generations, including Gen-

Z and Alphas. They unite under a shared purpose, embodying the spirit of community and compassion.

2021 Stats:[20]

Number of Chapters 224

Number of RFK Camps 180

Number of RFK Mentoring Programs 49

Number of States Represented 45

Number of Children Served at RFK Camp 8,876

Number of Children Served at RFK Mentoring................................ 802

Number of Adult Volunteers at RFK Camp.................................. 9,167

Number of Adult Volunteers at RFK Mentoring 1,216

Number of volunteer hours 776,371

Social Capital**.. $21,117,291.20

Returning RFK Alumni as

volunteers... 493

Adoptions resulting from Camp and/or Mentoring Programs

.... 9

Foster Parenting resulting from Camp and/or Mentoring

Programs.. 63

College Students who changed their course of study because of

service w/ RFK... 88

Since Inception

Total Campers served since 1985... 151,701

Total Volunteers serving since 1985 202,286

Dedication Defined: For The Children's Visionary Journey

What differentiates a clear vision from a murky one is its clarity of purpose. It's not merely about stating objectives but ensuring that every participant comprehends their role, responsibilities, and the larger picture they contribute to. It's this precise understanding that sets the stage for organizational excellence. True visions, when deeply rooted in passion and backed by decisive action, inevitably see triumphant realization.

In the case of For The Children, volunteers play a pivotal role. Despite no monetary rewards and the physical and emotional rigors of a week-long camp, they remain fully, passionately committed. The experience goes beyond mere participation - it's transformative for both volunteers and the children. For most, the rewards are deeply spiritual and emotional - a chance to be part of a noble vision, making a tangible difference in young lives.

Such profound engagement and consistent dedication have ensured that For The Children has thrived for over four decades. This isn't merely about providing camps for children. It's about instilling hope, reaffirming faith, and letting these children know they are important and loved. Volunteers don't just sympathize with these children; they empathize, providing them a genuine sense of family and belonging.

Many campers treasure their camp photo books - a testament to their transformative journey. These aren't just photos; they symbolize memories of a safe haven and the familial bonds they formed with volunteers. The positive ripples of this initiative are evident as many former campers, having turned their lives around, return as volunteers. They embody the living testament of For The Children's impact.

The organization's sustained success rests upon a clear vision shared passionately by its founders. Had this vision not been lucid and compelling, For The Children might have remained just a fleeting initiative. Instead, the founders' clear vision kindled a passionate drive in thousands of volunteers, making the organization a force for positive change.

Regular introspection and re-evaluation of the organizational vision is crucial. It should be an ongoing dialogue at all leadership levels, ensuring alignment with the overarching objectives. When vision is prioritized, it fosters increased engagement, paves the way for growth, and provides a clear direction for every action undertaken.

Innovation at Fairchild Semiconductor: Noyce's Legacy

In the 1950s, lifelong loyalty to a single employer was the norm, and the concept of frequent job shifts wasn't mainstream until the 1980s. So, when Bob Noyce and several colleagues left Shockley Semiconductor, it raised eyebrows. Their departure from a company that had wooed Noyce from across the country, and was founded by Nobel Prize winner Shockley, was seen as a significant betrayal. This group came to be known, somewhat derogatorily, as the "Traitorous Eight."[21]

Noyce left Shockley Semiconductor along with his Traitorous Eight colleagues in 1957 and soon after, founded Fairchild Semiconductor with the help of Sherman Fairchild and Arthur Rock (founder of Davis and Rock Venture Capital). The company they created became something special. Shunning traditional vertical management styles (which moved him to later found Intel) Noyce favored a collaborative approach. At this time, his goal was to build upon the transistor by jumping in with the team and a "roll your sleeves up" management philosophy. He preferred no office and decided to work in his cubicle, which happened to be no larger than anyone else's on the floor, which he liked to call the lab. In fact, people could not tell who was in charge of Fairchild when they visited — Noyce blended well.

Under Noyce's guidance, Fairchild Semiconductor cultivated a vibrant, inclusive culture, a rarity for that era. It attracted a diverse talent pool, including women, who were otherwise largely underrepresented in the workforce. The company's core hiring criteria revolved around capability, willingness, and passion. This openness and sense of purpose led team members to often work extended hours.

With a foundation of freedom, flexibility, and fiery drive quickly surfacing at Fairchild, creative ideas were a daily experience that hovered in many conversations throughout the office. Gatherings of people would happen without notice in the hallways, doorways, and cafeterias, with team members asking, "What if we did this?" or "What if we did that?" It was not uncommon to find Noyce stuck in the center of these gatherings. He found a nucleus of brilliance and excitement within the visits among peers and teammates.

During one of these gatherings, Jean A. Hoerni introduced Noyce to an idea that sounded contradictory to thought and theory. Hoerni called his idea the *planar process*. As usual, Noyce encouraged his team members to move on with projects and see where they led, unlike his then -rival, Shockley. He praised failure and with it, found success alongside an army of willing comrades helping him build something monumental.

The planar process is a manufacturing process, an idea Hoerni had developed earlier in 1957. However, it wasn't pursued until later, with a patent disclosure in January 1959. Within the transistor creation, the oxide layer was always thought to contaminate the silicon wafer but was left in place with the planar process to protect the p-n junctions. Simple as it may sound, this went against conventional wisdom. The planar process revolutionized transistor production and blew the doors open for new opportunities within the industry, also paving the way for Noyce's introduction of the integrated circuit.[22]

Noyce listened and promoted imaginative ideas from all teammates. Because of this mindset, the planar process exists, and yet another benchmark for technology was created setting the stage for radical technological inspiration.

Noyce's leadership style, which valued innovation and out-of-the-box thinking, meant that ideas like the planar process not only emerged but thrived. Such an environment underscored the significance of trusting teams to make decisions. It allowed team members the freedom to experiment, fail, learn, and innovate, aiming for the organization's collective growth.

Let people explore. Let them make mistakes. Let them talk through solutions and figure things out. Let them try new things and run with ideas. In essence, Fairchild Semiconductor's success under Noyce's leadership emphasized a key principle: to cultivate innovation, one must empower and trust the team, fostering an environment where exploration and calculated risks are not just tolerated but celebrated.

The Noyce Management System:

- Promote gatherings
- Listen
- Promote failure
- Everyone is on the same level in regard to conversation
- Imagine BIG
- Help each other grow
- And listen more

Although simple in context, this system is still considered leading-edge. Visions come in different settings and structures. To effectively incorporate this foundational approach, it must be rooted in the entity with complete consistency.

Marty Cagan, recognized as the primary thought leader for technology product management and founder of Product Group (SVPG) states in his book, INSPIRED, the following in regard to vision and innovation within the enterprise organization:

> *When the company was young, it likely had a clear and compelling vision. When it achieves the enterprise stage, however, the company has largely achieved that original vision and now people aren't sure what's next. Product teams complain about the lack of vision, lack of empowerment, the fact that it takes forever to get a decision made, and the product work is turning into design by committee.*

> *Leadership is likely frustrated, too, with the lack of innovation from the product teams. All too often, they resort to acquisitions or creating separate "innovation centers" to incubate new businesses in a protected environment. Yet this rarely results in the innovation they're so desperate for.*

Lack of vision is inherently an overriding issue among organizations in desperate need of creation and ingenuity. They find themselves struggling for the aggressiveness required for sustainability in vulnerable markets.[23]

Corporate Vision Statements

Raising Cane's

Raising Cane's, founded by Todd Graves in 1996, began with a simple idea: delivering the best chicken fingers. Guided by the principle that if you do one thing very well people will love it, Raising Cane's became an instant success. With over 600 restaurants as of 2022, Raising Cane's is doing much more than frying up the best chicken fingers in the business.

Raising Cane's Vision Statement:

> *"Our vision is to have locations all over the world and be known as the brand for quality chicken finger meals, a great crew, cool culture, and active community involvement."*[24]

Why is their chicken so good? Nothing is frozen—they receive the chicken fresh and cook it that day. They serve fresh fries, too, not pre-cut potatoes from a bag shipped from thousands of miles away. Nope—the fries are cut on location from real, fresh potatoes. These facts about the quality of their product are clearly stated on their website:

> *Quality is one of the main reasons everything we make tastes so great.*

Quality ingredients delivered and prepared fresh. Our standards are extremely high, and we like it that way. If your quality standards aren't as high, that's OK. After you eat here, they will skyrocket. And you'll thank us for it.

100% – We use 100% premium chicken tenderloins.

24 Hours – Our 24-hour marinade is one of the reasons our chicken fingers are so juicy.

Never-ever Frozen – Our chicken fingers are always fresh, never frozen. No exceptions.

They can check off goal #2 of the vision statement: Be known as the brand for quality chicken finger meals.

When walking into a Raising Cane's, you can't miss the bright colors or spirited energy of the staff who work there. You're there because you heard they have really good chicken fingers. Smiles and nice welcoming words greet you at every location. And if you're really wanting to have some fun, go through the drive-thru and hear the greeting, "Winner-winner, get your chicken dinner."

Goal #3 - met: a great crew and cool culture.

The last goal is active community involvement. This is one of the strongest statements of their vision, and they accomplish it with passion and vigor.

After founding Raising Cane's and building consistent growth, Todd Graves dove deep into what could be given back to the communities surrounding each restaurant. How do you establish a large business like Raising Cane's while developing strong community outreach? Two activities Graves initiated include:

1. <u>Community Partnerships</u> – The willingness to provide local support is one of the most important business ventures for Raising Cane's. They provide this support through a variety of fundraisers for education, feeding the hungry, pet welfare, and business development entrepreneurship.

2. Lemonade Day – This business development fundraiser was developed by Graves and his friend Michael Holthouse, along with Michael's daughter, Lissa. Lemonade Day was developed to teach young people to start early and learn the fundamentals of entrepreneurship in their own communities. Kids receive a backpack complete with workbooks covering how to build and market their own lemonade stand, lemonade recipes, and ideas on how to use revenue for savings and community involvement.

There you go—goal #4, active community involvement, accomplished.

It takes more than just a slogan thrown on the walls to make what Raising Cane's does every day successful. They live and breathe the vision, and it shows through the quality and values of the company and its team members.[25]

Simon Sinek Vision Statement / Sinek Partners

> *"I write about how to inspire action. I consult companies on how to build corporate cultures that inspire their team members. I guide companies on how to create marketing and communications that inspire customers to buy from them over and over and over. I speak to anyone who will listen. I work to be my own best-case study, practicing everything I preach."*[26]

Sinek does all of this in the books he's authored, and the TED Talks he's given. His ability to connect with his audience through his followers and staff at Sinek Partners proves this vision statement and says it all. The vision statement empowers all Sinek partners.

1. **Inspire Action** – His books and TED Talks inspire thought that pushes his audience into quick action.
2. **Consult companies to inspire team members** – Sinek pushes corporations to inject more inspiration into their team members by teaching them to become leaders, as opposed to mere managers.

3. **Inspire customers to buy over and over and over** – This is not popular or politically correct phrasing, but it states, "over and over and over." team members are well versed in this simple concept and understand the plan.
4. **Speak to anyone** – This implies that it doesn't matter who is in the audience: young, old, poor, successful, Black, Caucasian, Hispanic, Asian, etc. Sinek and his team will talk to anyone to accomplish point #1—inspire action!
5. **Work to be the best-case study, practicing everything preached** – Powerful! This is where it's at—working from the top down. Simon Sinek works the plan he writes for others. He understands that words inspire the possibility to move mountains, while action makes the difference.

Sinek says he holds himself accountable to five guiding principles to realize his vision:

1. **Be unconventional:** Shake things up. Offer new perspectives. Only when you see or hear things in a different way can you see greater opportunities.
2. **Keep it simple:** If people can more easily understand something, then it's more likely to get done.
3. **Collaborate:** Work with others because they know more and have already made all the mistakes.
4. **Silver-line it:** Look for the silver lining in every cloud. It's better to amplify what works than be obsessed with fixing what doesn't work.
5. **Act!:** Action is always better than inaction.[27]

Catalina Foothills School District, Tucson, AZ

Our Vision: Learning transfers to life beyond the Catalina Foothills School District experience, enabling each student to flourish as a responsible citizen in the global community.

Our Mission: Catalina Foothills School District, a caring and collaborative learning community, ensures that each student achieves intellectual and personal excellence, and is well prepared for college and career pathways.[28]

When school administrators, faculty, and staff focus solely on a vision or mission statement, they risk missing the bigger picture. Hayes Mizell, Director of the Program for Student Achievement at the Edna McConnell Clark Foundation, highlighted this issue when he told Education World... "I think the major problem with most mission statements is that they are static. They seem to say, at best, 'This is who we are. This is what we do. This is what we value.' But if one believes, as I do, that most schools need to improve, such a statement merely affirms what the school is rather than what it *should be*."[29]

Many institutions struggle due to their vision, mission, and values (VMV) not being clearly articulated or understood. A slight deviation can, over time, lead them significantly astray. However, realigning the VMV can transform them into a cohesive force, driving the institution towards its aspirational goals.

Mizell further argued that "many mission statements have little practical meaning" and while "are posted on walls and in the student handbook or scheduler, but they rarely guide or challenge the school. They are too safe and too easily forgotten. Even in the best circumstances, the mission statement is often one more good intention pushed to the background." Even in the best circumstances, the mission statement can fade into the backdrop, becoming just another good intention.

Consider Virginia Beach City Public Schools. Their vision is "to see that every student achieves their maximum potential." Such a vision commits the institution to the success of each student, challenging teachers, staff, and administrators to push boundaries. By striving for this vision, excellence permeates classrooms, hallways, and even lunchrooms - surrounding the school's entirety with purpose and drive. It's a call to action for teachers by challenging them to deeply engage with each student, nurturing their potential from the outset. The chain reaction of this commitment benefits everyone, from the individual student to the global community.

The vision is the macro-target, and the missions are the micro-actions. These eventually and inevitably hit the mark to establish values, promoting the growth of all involved.

How BIG Is Your Vision?

Is your vision BIG enough or just basic? Is your vision a motivator that removes any obstacle? Will it stand the test of time like the visions of Disney, FedEx, and others, even through the ups and downs?

Does your vision have the future insight for an infinity of greatness?

The word average is an adjective defined on Dictionary.com as typical; common; ordinary. Does your group's vision strive to hit beyond the typical, common, or ordinary? Is your team driven to set your sights on more than the ordinary, conquer the unimaginable, and realize the full potential of your business, organization, team, and people, and yourself?

Why Not An Audacious And Extreme Vision?

When Wilbur and Orville Wright thought of their vision, it was extreme. Their ambition was seen as both audacious and radical. To think a small bicycle company could think BIG - like that, but they pursued their goals anyway. Their vision was massive. That's what got them up every day for three years. What about the vision of having a phone that someone could swipe across the screen to open and use for a million different purposes, from financing to entertainment? Steve Jobs thought so. What about the creation of a new exploration company to not just match, but now exceed NASA? Elon Musk, Sir Richard Branson, and Jeff Bezos think so. It should be a comfort, but certainly not without challenges along the way, that it only takes one individual to start the belief. Will it be you?

Is the vision for your establishment too small? If so, be careful—someone just might one-up your vision and overtake your niche. There might be a company being formed that will auspiciously overtake the market in which you now excel, designing the next technology that will make yours irrelevant because they're thinking of a massively big audacious vision. Remember that without a vision, the people will perish. Go BIG with your vision and thrive.

Questions To Ponder:

1. *What* is the vision?
2. Is the vision *BIG* enough?
3. Do our people *know* the vision?
4. Do our people *really understand* the vision?
5. Do our people know their *place* in the vision?
6. Do we work *daily* in the direction of physically realizing the vision?
7. Is there a real *plan* to accomplish the vision?
8. What do I need *to do* better to see the vision through?

Virgin Atlantic Vision Statement:

Our vision at Virgin Atlantic is to be the most loved travel company and what drives this is the power of human connection, both between our people and our customers.[30]

Mission

He will win whose army is animated by the same spirit throughout all its ranks.

Sun Tzu, The Art of War

Mission – a special assignment that is given to a person or group. (thefreedictionary.com)

Mission statement – an official document that sets out the goals, purpose, and work of an organization. (dictionary.com)

Origin of The Mission Statement:

While at Shockley Semiconductor, Noyce quickly realized that Shockley wouldn't grant him the autonomy or flexibility he needed to fully harness the potential of the transistor. Although their primary objective was to innovate using the transistor, Noyce and his team sensed that their creative ideas would be consistently dissected and criticized under Shockley's micromanagement. The atmosphere was electric; the brightest minds in the industry were brainstorming tirelessly. With ample funding and a talented team, they were positioned to develop groundbreaking products for the future. And having the prestigious "Shockley" label seemed like the perfect finishing touch. How could such an ideal setup be doomed?

On paper, Shockley Semiconductor seemed destined for greatness. But as its reputation and resources expanded, internal tensions began to surface. Despite his intellectual prowess, Shockley was proving to be a poor leader. Top-down leadership can stifle innovation and momentum, especially when the conveyed vision starts to lose its clarity. While the overarching goal was to revolutionize the semiconductor sector, the roadmap to achieve it was becoming increasingly hazy.

A mission, by definition, is a special assignment that is given to a person or group. The mission at Shockley started to crumble as Shockley's attention turned increasingly insular. With the shift in focus, the momentum that had been driving the team began to dissipate. Surprisingly, despite having all the tools for success, the venture seemed destined to falter.[31]

Countless times we have seen the perfect setup for success fail miserably due to vision and mission being distorted, forgotten, or simply abandoned.

History is replete with examples of ventures with all the makings of success faltering due to a loss of clarity or commitment to their vision and mission. The dot-com bubble in the late '90s stands as a testament. Visionaries were inundated with billions in investments, but many floundered because of leadership's inability to pursue their mission with the same enthusiasm as their vision. A similar trajectory was observed in 2022 with the boom and subsequent downturn of non-fungible token (NFT) adoption and trading. Without leadership that can clearly define and champion a mission, the foundation becomes unstable. While funding is oxygen to a startup's survival, robust leadership is the keystone to its success.

Ashland Chemical

Ashland Global Holdings revenue through March 31, 2022, topped $2.250B, a 21.62 percent increase year-over-year and a current market value of $5.601.9B.

Old Mission Statement

We are a market-focused, process-centered organization that develops and delivers innovative solutions to our customers, consistently outperforms our peers, produces predictable earnings for our shareholders, and provides a dynamic and challenging environment for our employees.

New Mission Statement

We satisfy our customers by delivering results through quality chemical products and services. Our desire to grow drives our passion to win in the marketplace. With a unified, low-cost operating structure, we'll remain competitive across every business and in every geographic region.

The choice to transition from the previous statement that boasted "consistently outperforms our peers" was a judicious one. Encouraging competition amongst peers within a mission can undermine collaborative efforts. On the other hand, championing a "passion to win in the marketplace" has the potential to galvanize teams and entire organizations. It allows individuals to embrace and reflect the mission in their daily endeavors. A mission encapsulates the consistent efforts - hourly, daily, weekly, monthly, and annually - directed towards realizing the vision.

Take, for instance, a Fortune 500 company with the mission statement "ensure profitability for our stockholders." This only captures the objective for a single financial quarter. A mission should encapsulate a broader commitment, guiding any team member or company initiative to fruition. Imagine if mission statements focused solely on immediate actions to inch closer to the overarching vision. In such a scenario, the Vision-Mission-Values (VMV) framework might appear quite different.

- **Vision** – Where the company wants to go. (The Future)
- **Mission** – The tasks at hand to see the vision through. (The Present)
- **Values** – How we realize the mission through our character. (The Foundation)

The prestige of a name alone can't sustain a mission's integrity. While Shockley's name attracted attention and brought together eight brilliant minds in one place, it was insufficient to maintain cohesion. Merely having a mission statement on a website, displayed on a wall, or printed on letterhead is commendable, but it's not fully effective unless it's deeply ingrained in the mindset, heart, and rationale of every team member. This is particularly true for those in leadership positions, as they are the catalysts behind the organization.

Let's look at a "Sample" School Vision Statement:

One of the biggest challenges with Vision and Mission is the clear separation between both.

- Our instruction will be differentiated and lead to the success of the whole student.
- Our child-centered environment will be safe and positive to support student learning, growth, and development.
- Our staff will create a supportive environment that promotes collaboration, reflection, and ongoing professional growth with a unified focus on student success.
- Our school will engage the community to work together and share the responsibility of educating students through effective means of communication and engagement.[32]

Though these statements are constructive and are categorized under "vision," they function more like daily objectives or missions. These principles might be more fitting under the school's mission, emphasizing daily behaviors and standards to uphold. Additionally, transitioning these statements from future to present tense could create a more immediate and actionable impact. A mission statement like this can pave the way for a grander vision.

To clarify the distinction between vision and mission statements, it's essential to understand their individual meanings and then contextualize each appropriately.

Company Mission Statements

Disney's Mission Statement:

Disney's 2012 mission statement:

"Make people happy" (Walt Disney Archives, 2012)

Disney's mission statement today:

> *"To entertain, inform and inspire people around the globe through the power of unparalleled storytelling, reflecting the iconic brands, creative minds and innovative technologies that make ours the world's premier entertainment company."*

Disney's current mission encompasses every one of its vast array of businesses — from Pixar, ESPN, Maker Studios, History Channel, to Marvel Entertainment, LucasFilm, and Vice Media. The intent is to provide every entity under the Disney umbrella a voice. At the core, all these companies deliver one primary thing: entertainment. And what is the essence of good entertainment? It educates, updates, influences, and perhaps most crucially, especially for a brand synonymous with joy like Walt Disney, it brings happiness. The real challenge lies in conveying this sentiment to teams beyond the boardrooms and legal departments, ensuring every cast member understands that their day-to-day endeavors aim to spread happiness via Disney's mission.

So, what do Disney staff need to internalize to spread joy? The mission to "entertain, inform, and inspire people..." is not just the rationale for Disney's existence but the methodology as well. For this mission to translate into actionable results, it must be clear, relatable, and straightforward enough for every team member (or 'cast member' in Disney parlance) across all Disney's subsidiaries. They should easily articulate and embody it. If the overarching objective is to spread happiness, then the organization should always act in harmony with the very audience they cater to.

Bob Iger's ascendancy to the CEO position in 2005 had a clear directive: to solidify Disney's footprint in the global media landscape. An immediate and pivotal step in this direction was the acquisition of Pixar. At the point of Iger's takeover, due to differences between the then-CEO Michael Eisner and Pixar, it appeared that the Disney-Pixar collaboration had reached its finale. However, not long after his appointment, Iger initiated dialogue with Steve Jobs about the audacious idea of purchasing Pixar. The primary concern for Pixar was the potential dilution of their innovative edge under Disney's traditionalist approach. Ingeniously, Iger orchestrated the acquisition in a manner that it almost seemed like Pixar was, in spirit, acquiring Disney Animation by placing Pixar's John Lasseter and Edwin Catmull at the helm of Disney Productions. This strategic move ensured that both Disney and Pixar continued to evolve and produce premium content, aligning with their greater mission.

In essence, Disney's mission serves as a beacon guiding them towards their vision. They understand that the ultimate manifestation of excellent entertainment is the happiness it brings to its audience. Through a three-faceted approach outlined in their mission, Disney remains committed to realizing their 2012 vision of "making people happy."

1. Entertain, inform, and inspire people around the globe through unparalleled storytelling.
2. Reflect iconic (traditional and historic) brands.
3. Have creative minds and innovative technologies to advance entertainment.

Consider Disney's stated corporate vision: "To be one of the world's leading producers and providers of entertainment and information."

At the end of the day, the goal of the vision and the mission statement is to work in harmony throughout the organization. Disney is moving further away from the primary focus of making us happy because there is a significant focus on "entertainment and information." With acquisitions of iconic brands including Pixar, Marvel, ABC, Hulu, and Fox, Disney continues to build an empire that is becoming the world leader in entertainment and information, yet, in the end, the immediate threat is losing sight of its main pillar – making people happy.[33]

Google's Mission Statement:

"To organize the world's information and make it universally accessible and useful."[34]

Google has also posted "Ten things we know to be true." Google states the truth of the HOW within the following ten items:

1. Focus on the user and all else will follow.
2. It's best to do one thing really, really well.
3. Fast is better than slow.
4. Democracy on the web works.
5. You don't need to be at your desk to need an answer.
6. You can make money without doing evil.
7. There's always more information out there.
8. The need for information crosses all borders.
9. You can be serious without a suit.
10. Great just isn't good enough.[35]

Harvard Business Review stated the following:

> *The goal of a brand is to communicate a distinctive value proposition to a specific set of customers. Consumers made Google the top search engine because it was the best product, not because of the company's social mission to "organize the world's information."*[36]

While the product certainly drew customers in, it was Google's mission to "organize the world's information" that truly resonated and ensured consistent product delivery. This mission wasn't just met—it was surpassed, leading to the rise of the phrase, *"Did you Google it?"* whenever someone referred to an online search. Google's strategy was to transform its brand name, originally a noun, into a widely used verb, a linguistic transformation known as "anthimeria." This was achieved through laser-focused dedication.

At a time when other search engines cluttered their homepages with various content in 1995, Google showcased a simple, yet very noticeable, search bar at the center of their landing page. They recognized that users wanted a streamlined search experience, not an overloaded, *People Magazine style* portal. Staying true to this insight, Google prioritized two core philosophies: *"Focus on the user and all else will follow"* and *"It's best to do one thing really, really well."*

Many organizations today grapple with a loss of focus. In the modern business landscape, embedding the Vision, Mission, and Values (VMV) in every operational aspect is imperative. VMV should encapsulate the entire organization's spirit. When genuinely integrated, it becomes a living entity, spurring organic growth that can surpass expectations, much like Google's trajectory. Google's unyielding commitment to its mission—effectively organizing the world's information—sets them apart. If they maintain this trajectory of excellence, they'll undoubtedly realize what many speculate to be their vision: providing the world's information at a single click.[37]

Amazon's Mission Statement:

> *"To be Earth's most customer-centric company where people can find and discover anything they want to buy online."*

Amazon Leadership Principles:

- Customer Obsession
- Ownership
- Invent and Simplify
- Are Right, A Lot
- Hire and Develop the Best
- Insist on the Highest Standards
- Think Big
- Bias for Action
- Frugality

- Vocally Self Critical
- Earn Trust of Others
- Dive Deep
- Have Backbone; Disagree and Commit
- Deliver Results[38]

Amazon possesses an uncanny knack for consistently hitting the mark. In 2021, they catered to over 300 million customers, raking in more than $400 billion—a striking 21 percent increase from the previous year. They've not only set records but shattered them, becoming the fastest-growing company in history. Their Prime subscription alone soared past 200 million members in 2021. These figures clearly show that Amazon's mission statement isn't just words on paper; it's the core driving force behind their monumental success.

What sets Amazon apart is how they delineate their mission. They don't just state it; they break it down into actionable tenets through their Amazon Leadership Principles.

In essence, Amazon's ethos communicates, "Our guiding star is an unwavering obsession with customer satisfaction. We don't just take responsibility; we own it. We constantly innovate, simplifying processes to enhance efficiency. Our track record of success is no accident; we prioritize hiring top-tier talent and uphold rigorous standards. We foster an environment where thinking big isn't just encouraged—it's expected. And when it comes to taking action, we believe in walking the talk. We're prudent with our resources, treating every penny as if it were our last. Recognizing our missteps and learning from them is part of our DNA. Dependability isn't just a word to us—it's a commitment. We believe in thorough research and finding holistic solutions. Standing up for what's right, even when it's tough, is a principle we hold dear. And at the end of the day, our focus is unerringly on driving results."

Chipotle's Mission Statement:

> *"Our focus has always been on using higher-quality ingredients and cooking techniques to make great food accessible to all people at reasonable prices. But our vision has evolved. While using a variety of fresh ingredients remains the foundation of our menu, we believe that "fresh is not enough anymore." Now we want to know the sources for all our ingredients, so that we can be sure they are as flavorful as possible while we are mindful of the environmental and societal impact of our business. We call this idea, Food With Integrity, and it guides how we run our business."*[39]

Chipotle's mission statement is both thoughtfully constructed and reflective of their core values. Yet, it's common for companies to clutter their vision, mission, and values with unnecessary detail. Adhering to the principle that "less is more," a succinct mission statement often resonates more powerfully. In its mission, Chipotle delves into particulars, emphasizing the significance of each ingredient they serve.

However, Chipotle's reputation took a hit when E.coli outbreaks were linked to several of their outlets. Their robust company principles enabled a swift recovery, driven by revamped processes and a recommitment to their foundational values. This ordeal underscored the pitfalls when an organization's vision, mission, and values are not effectively communicated, embedded in staff training, or embodied by its leaders. Leaders play a pivotal role in interpreting and upholding the VMV, ensuring consistent practices that yield predictable positive customer outcomes instead of detrimental ones. Such an orientation exemplifies a proactive stance rather than a mere reactive one.

While Chipotle is a commendable company with an inspiring journey, challenges can arise even in the best organizations. It's evident that without ongoing education, skills development, and reinforcement of core values, organizations open themselves to misunderstandings, leading to unforeseen challenges.

Below is the "open letter" apology by Chipotle CEO Steve Ells:

> *Since I opened the first Chipotle more than 23 years ago, we have strived to elevate fast food by using better ingredients which are raised responsibly, without synthetic hormones, antibiotics, added colors, flavors or sweeteners typically found in processed fast food. And I'm very proud of that.*
>
> *But in 2015, we failed to live up to our own food safety standards, and in doing so, we let our customers down. At that time, I made a promise to all our customers that we would elevate our food safety program.*
>
> *HERE ARE THE IMPORTANT CHANGES WE MADE:*
>
> 1. *Supplier Interventions Our suppliers have implemented additional, proven steps that eliminate or dramatically reduce food safety risks before the ingredients ever reach Chipotle.*
> 2. *Advanced Technology We are pioneering advanced technologies including using high pressure to eliminate any possible food safety issues without changing the flavor of the ingredients.*
> 3. *Farmer Support & Training We are providing funding and training to local farms so they can meet our elevated food safety requirements.*
> 4. *Enhanced Restaurant Procedures We deployed robust, industry leading new food safety procedures in our restaurants including new handling procedures for produce, citrus, and meats as well as comprehensive sanitizing protocols.*
> 5. *Food Safety Certification We require that our managers and field leaders are certified in food safety by a nationally recognized institution - a first for any national restaurant chain.*

6. *Restaurant Inspections We dramatically increased the number, and intensity, of restaurant inspections - both by independent auditors and our internal teams.*

7. *Ingredient Traceability We implemented an advanced electronic tracking system to ensure that ingredients can be monitored and quickly removed from our supply if necessary.*

8. *Advisory Council We created an independent advisory council comprised of industry experts who continually review our procedures and provide insight into new food safety advancements.*

Our commitment to you is that every day, in every restaurant, we will serve food that is safe, delicious, and made with ingredients raised with care.

I never could have imagined that one burrito restaurant would become the company it is today. On behalf of our entire team, we look forward to continuing with you on our quest to make better food accessible to everyone.

Steve Ells Founder, Chairman & Co-CEO

Details at chipotle.com/foodsafety.[40,41]

Ells' letter clearly outlines the failures that occurred and subsequently presents the detailed steps the organization took to achieve the predictable outcome they desired.

Bridgewater Associates, LP:

Bridgewater Associates, with $150 billion in global investments, collaborates with over 350 of the world's most sophisticated institutions as of 2022. The core belief of the company hinges on a profound level of transparency, unparalleled in most business environments.

Initiated by Ray Dalio, Bridgewater boasts approximately 1,700 team members globally, of which 1,400 are based in Connecticut.

In *Originals*, Adam Grant offers an intriguing portrayal of Bridgewater's distinct approach to business transparency. He cites an email from a client advisor directed at Ray Dalio. This communication, devoid of flattery, is stark in its candor.

> *"Ray— you deserve a 'D-' for your performance today...you meandered for 50 minutes...It was evident to all of us that there was a lack of preparation on your part. Given that we've earmarked this prospect as a 'must-win', today's performance was disappointing...we can't afford a repeat."*[42]

In many corporate landscapes, such directness might spell career doom. However, Dalio not only internalized the feedback but also shared it with the entire company. This move underscored the message that everyone, irrespective of their rank, should be committed to excellence and embrace transparency wholeheartedly.

Bridgewater doesn't lean on a conventional mission statement. Instead, they're steered by over two hundred "Principles." These guidelines not only shape their daily endeavors and client solutions but also streamline decision-making.

Dalio published the "Principles" in 2017 and also provided a free downloadable book on bridgewater.com describing each in detail. While Dalio describes them as mere guiding thoughts, they have resonated deeply. With over two million downloads at the time of this account, it's evident that many value this trove of openness and radical candor.

Bridgewater's Top 20 Principles:

1. Trust in truth.
2. Realize that you have nothing to fear from truth.
3. Create an environment in which everyone has the right to understand what makes sense and no one has the right to hold a critical opinion without speaking up about it.
4. Be extremely open.
5. Have integrity and demand it from others.
    a. Never say anything about the person you wouldn't say to them directly, and don't try people without accusing them to their face.
    b. Don't let "loyalty" stand in the way of truth and openness.
6. Be radically transparent. Record almost all meetings and share them with all relevant people.
7. Don't tolerate dishonesty.
8. Don't believe it when someone caught being dishonest says they have seen the light and will never do that sort of thing again.
9. Create a culture in which it is OK to make mistakes but unacceptable not to identify, analyze, and learn from them.
10. Recognize that effective, innovative thinkers are going to make mistakes.
11. Do not feel bad about your mistakes or those of others. Love them!
12. Observe the patterns of mistakes to see if they are a product of weaknesses.
13. Do not feel bad about your weaknesses or those of others.
14. Don't worry about looking good – worry about achieving your goals.
15. Get over "blame" and "credit" and get on with "accurate" and "inaccurate."
16. Don't depersonalize mistakes.
17. Write down your weaknesses and the weaknesses of others to help remember and acknowledge them.

18. When you experience pain, remember to reflect.
19. Be self-reflective and make sure your people are self-reflective.
20. Teach and reinforce the merits of mistake-based learning. The most valuable tool we have for this is the issues log, which is aimed at identifying and learning from mistakes.[43]

Dalio's pioneering "Principles" are more than just guidelines; they form the very DNA of Bridgewater Associates. Comprising 210 principles in total, each is meticulously crafted and is far from mere words on a page. These principles define the operational methodology at Bridgewater.

Dalio's personal commitment to these principles is evident. His willingness to share a candid, critical email with the entire company underscores his deep investment in these guidelines and his belief in transparency and continuous improvement.

Contrary to the hierarchical structures seen in many organizations, where the top echelon dictates values and practices, Bridgewater flips the script. Every team member, from the C-suite to the newest recruit, is expected to align their behavior, communication, and decisions with the "Principles." This cohesive commitment ensures that the company's mission is perpetually supported and realized.

Of all the principles, one particularly stands out: dedicated transparency. While many organizations pay lip service to this ideal, Dalio has made it an integral aspect of Bridgewater's culture. He doesn't just advocate for radical honesty; he embodies it. This is exemplified in his decision to share a critical email with the entire team. It prompts the question: How many leaders would truly have the courage to do the same?

The Virgin Atlantic Mission Statement:

> *"Our mission statement is simple, yet the foundation of everything we do here at Virgin Atlantic Airways... to embrace the human spirit and let it fly."*

Richard Branson, the iconic founder and brand ambassador of Virgin Atlantic Airways, has steered the airline to become one of the world's most recognizable brands. Their mission is beautifully simple yet profound: "to embrace the human spirit and let it fly."

This sentiment encapsulates the essence of what work should feel like. It's not just a slogan but a way of life at Virgin. Virgin's members likely resonate deeply with this philosophy because it's invigorating and fun! This mission, with its passionate and memorable words, is essentially a motivational speech, inspiring every individual who wants to thrive and "let it fly."

Every day, this mission is the guiding directive for Virgin's team members. They internalize it, and it's evident to their guests. It's a compelling, concise, and powerful statement that perfectly aligns with the company's broader vision. It prompts team members to be proud, embrace their unique personalities, elevate the Virgin experience, and radiate enthusiasm and joy to everyone aboard, be it fellow teammate or passenger.

Regular reflection to ensure alignment between one's vision and mission is essential. When they harmonize, the impact is unparalleled.[44]

Trader Joe's Mission Statement:[45]

> *"To give our customers the best food and beverage values that they can find anywhere and to provide them with the information required to make informed buying decisions. We provide these with a dedication to the highest quality of customer satisfaction delivered with a sense of warmth, friendliness, fun, individual pride, and company spirit."*

Trader Joe's mission is clear and differentiated right from the outset. By mentioning their customers in the opening line, they highlight their paramount importance. The mission doesn't merely claim to provide "the best food"; such a general statement might invite skepticism. Instead, they focus on delivering the best "food and beverage values." This precision situates them favorably against other competitors in the market. It resonates in the minds of both customers and team members, reinforcing the perception of Trader Joe's as a brand committed to value.

Since its inception in 1958, Trader Joe's has consistently emphasized value. The brand's commitment to offering top-quality products traces back to the foundational values instilled by its founder, Joe Coulombe.

Coulombe began his venture by acquiring a chain of convenience stores named Pronto Markets in the 1950s. However, recognizing a market gap for fresh, quality groceries, he pivoted, giving birth to the first Trader Joe's store. The grocery market was craving innovation and quality, and Coulombe was poised to deliver. Decades later, that commitment remains steady. Their mission, as detailed under the "About Us" section on their website, attests to this enduring dedication.

> *We understood then, as we do today, that maintaining our everyday focus on Value is vital, which is why we don't have sales, loyalty programs, membership fees, or any other gimmicks. Instead, here is what we do:*
>
> - *We buy directly from suppliers whenever possible; we bargain hard to get the best price, and then pass the savings on to you.*
> - *If an item doesn't pull its weight in our stores, it goes away to the gangway for something else.*
> - *We buy in volume and contract early to get the best prices.*
> - *Most grocers charge their suppliers fees for putting an item on the shelf. This results in higher prices... so we don't do it.*
> - *We keep our costs low—because every penny we save is a penny you save.*
>
> *Confidence builds in team members' minds when they understand that providing the best food and beverage values is their duty. Knowing this encourages a higher sense of passion to deliver the mission that customers experience every day through the expressions and vibe of Trader Joe's team members.*[46]

Zappos' Mission Statement:

The mission statement of Zappos, also referred to by partner team members as their "WOW Philosophy," is: "To provide the best customer service possible."

"Wow" definition:

Verb: to gain an enthusiastic response from; thrill.

Noun: an extraordinary success.[47,48]

Zappos is one of the strongest customer-centered companies existing today. They write their narrative with a simple mission statement: "To provide the best customer service possible."

Then Zappos follows that up with an explanation found in the Ten Family Core Values. The Zappos mission statement philosophy and Family Core Values work hand-in-hand, and everyone in the company contributes to the values annually:

1. Deliver WOW Through Service
2. Embrace and Drive Change
3. Create Fun and A Little Weirdness
4. Be Adventurous, Creative, and Open-Minded
5. Pursue Growth and Learning
6. Build Open and Honest Relationships With Communication
7. Build a Positive Team and Family Spirit
8. Do More With Less
9. Be Passionate and Determined
10. Be Humble

Zappos' Best Customer Service:

What's the true price of exceptional customer service? Zappos is frequently lauded for its unparalleled customer-centric approach. So much so, they've developed their own training program for other companies eager to emulate their success. Many businesses would do well to prioritize customer service as Zappos does.

They understand the full cycle from order placement to delivery and foster a culture where every team member is devoted to enhancing customer experience. They continually evaluate their approach, asking whether their level of customer service will support sustained, profitable growth. As we'll delve deeper later in this book, Zappos emerges as a company worthy of in-depth analysis and emulation. Crucially, their mission is not just a statement; it's backed by a concrete action plan.

Nordstrom's Commitment:

In store or online, wherever new opportunities arise, Nordstrom works relentlessly to give customers the most compelling shopping experience possible. The one constant? John W. Nordstrom's founding philosophy: "offer the customer the best possible service, selection, quality and value."[49]

Nordstrom's understanding of customer service is evident from the outset of their commitment statement: "In store or online, wherever new opportunities arise." Regardless where the business is coming from, now or in the future, they work to provide the customer the very best experience possible. This isn't just about transactions; it's about crafting an "experience," ensuring each interaction is memorable and personalized.

The guiding question seems to be, "What would John Nordstrom do?" His vision, centered on superior service, selection, quality, and value, differentiates the brand in a marketplace increasingly driven by fleeting interactions and cost-cutting. Unlike many modern companies that distance themselves from their founders' principles, Nordstrom proudly anchors its mission in its heritage. This history reinforces the distinction between mere interaction and a genuine experience.

As many long-standing businesses lean towards impersonal interactions and mass-produced items with less-than perfect quality, Nordstrom's mission statement reminds team members the philosophy of their founder and offers customers the best possible service, selection, quality, and value. Nordstrom's commitment doesn't say the lowest price. It says value. This might manifest in a thoughtful gesture, an unexpected thank you note, or an act of going beyond what's expected. Such commitment to detail not only elevates the customer experience but also enriches the company's reputation. There's unparalleled satisfaction in witnessing a team embodying these principles, consistently going the extra mile in both big gestures and small nuances.

HubSpot:

Vision Statement

- We commit maniacally to both our mission and metrics.
- We look to the long-term and Solve for The Customer.
- We share openly and are remarkably transparent.
- We favor autonomy and take ownership.
- We believe our best perk is amazing people.
- We dare to be different and question the status quo.
- We recognize that life is short.

Mission Statement

"HubSpot helps millions of organizations grow better, and we'd love to grow better with you. Our business builds the software and systems that power the world's small to medium-sized businesses.

Our company culture builds connections, careers, and employee growth. How? By creating a workplace that values flexibility, autonomy, and transparency. If that sounds like something you'd like to be part of, we'd love to hear from you. You can find out more about our company culture in the HubSpot Culture Code, which has more than 3M views, and learn about our commitment to creating a diverse and inclusive workplace, too."

Values

- Humble
- Empathetic
- Adaptable
- Remarkable
- Transparent

HubSpot's vision leans towards what typically characterizes a mission, emphasizing immediate objectives and strategies. Conversely, their mission seems more attuned to career development and long-term growth. While HubSpot's values are identifiable, a clear definition for each would provide an even deeper level of clarity in how each should be embodied and executed more effectively in the day-to-day setting.[50, 51]

Richard Branson on Crafting Your Mission Statement:

Clarity and brevity are essential. Consider the 140-character template from X (formerly Twitter) when crafting your guiding message. This concise message should clarify your company's intent and set expectations for both internal and external stakeholders. Make it specific to your company, memorable, authentic, and for an imaginative touch, envision it as the motto on a coat of arms.[52]

When examining vision, mission, and values, the mission often seems ambiguous. Dictionary.com describes a mission statement as a formal declaration of an organization's core purpose and objectives. Yet, in many cases, this has been conflated with the vision statement, causing confusion regarding the true essence of the mission.

Missions are dynamic. They can shift weekly, monthly, or annually. This fluidity reinforces their importance. To maintain their relevance, missions must remain at the forefront of every team member's mind. If neglected, a mission's credibility can wane, leading to misconceptions, obsolescence, and inconsistency. This can ripple outwards, destabilizing company culture and blurring its vision.

Fully grasp the mission and embody it. Ensure all team members understand and can articulate it at any given moment. Craft a mission that is clear, direct, and resonates with every team member. Ambiguous statements can cause confusion. Avoid relegating the mission to a mere afterthought. When aligned with the mission, team members can enact it daily, ensuring it's not just a decorative phrase but a living principle.

A mission matters when it resonates deeply, carries significance, and is consistently actionable. It should drive action, not confusion. Often, missions get buried under complex, irrelevant wording, detached from the company's overarching vision. To realize a vision, establish a robust mission statement, anchored by a firm set of values. With collective commitment to the Vision-Mission-Values (VMV) framework, transformative results become attainable. Through unified effort and clarity of purpose, organizations can transcend the ordinary and achieve the extraordinary.

The reality is that a company's mission needs to translate into real, active execution.

Mission Confusion

A Green Beret once commented to the global news agency, Reuters, about the ambiguity of direction in the military, particularly concerning the rules of engagement in Afghanistan. He remarked:

> *"What happens when failure to provide clear guidance with missions is that it creates moral cowardice, and with a vague mission it produces an ability to reap the rewards of success without facing the responsibility of failure."*

The danger of mission ambiguity is profound. Its ongoing effects can permeate every facet of an operation, from top to bottom and across all departments. This confusion can undermine even the most efficient of organizations, and in swift measure, topple giants – even institutions as formidable as the U.S. military. Hence, crafting a clear, well-understood, and meticulously planned mission is paramount. If a mission isn't comprehensive, coherent, and communicated effectively from the beginning, it's already compromised and needs to be re-delivered to ensure alignment across all stakeholders.

Mission In Chaos

May 22, 2011, began as a typical Sunday with church services, graduation ceremonies, weddings, and afternoon lunch for the people in Joplin, Missouri. What started with calm ended in disbelief and tragedy for the community of 51,000 residents.

At 5:14 p.m., the National Weather Service issued the alarm that an EF1 tornado was heading toward Joplin. Unfortunately, several thousand residents who needed to hear the sound did not. As the wind tunnel pushed through outlying communities, the intensity increased from an EF1 to an EF2 (113-157 mph) within minutes. Continuing to make its half (later three-quarter) mile wide way down the path, the tornado eventually hit EF5 (260-318 mph) status before striking the core of Joplin.

Joplin, which is a part of Jasper County, averages twenty-five weather watches a year. Of those, there are approximately eighteen severe thunderstorms and seven floor tornados. Of the twenty-five weather watches, sirens are activated on average once a year, or 4 percent of the time. Historically, the tornados for which sirens have been activated in Joplin have been rated EF0 through EF2, with the occasional EF3 thrown in. Less than one half of one percent result in EF5 tornadoes. All EF5s that have been recorded were those in Oklahoma City, Oklahoma; Greensburg, Kansas; and Joplin. Keith Stammer, Director of Joplin Emergency Management, said, "This is not something that we were expecting. With tornadic activity, you're always up for it but nothing of this level."

At 5:34 p.m., the EF5 devastation began to unravel as deadly 200 mph-plus winds ripped through homes and buildings as if they were made of straw. Cars and trucks whirled through the air like tin cans, and once the thirty-eight minutes of howling destruction ended, Joplin looked flat, empty, and utterly destroyed. The aftermath of confusion hit hard and fast.

With sirens blaring, emergency vehicles scrambled to find the nearest rescue mission. Mass havoc settled in quickly, and many life-saving missions began to take shape.

Stammer recalled going down to the Emergency Operations Center that afternoon around 1:30 p.m. to watch dispatch, listen to radio traffic, and visit with his team about the activity to ensure what was happening. Later in the day, there was a warning report of a tornado heading their way. However, "that one turned and went north towards Webb City in that direction and did not at all look like it was going to intersect with Joplin." The policy is to activate the sirens if there is a tornado in the vicinity or a portion of the city.

The report of tornadic activity came in from the west edge of town, and Stammer activated the sirens. KZRG Radio did a simulcast for bad weather and called Stammer to ask what was happening when the sirens were sounding. What follows is the conversion between Stammer and KZRG: "...we understand the sirens are going on, why is that?" I said, "Well we have a report of a tornado that's headed this way, so we've activated the sirens." At that point, Stammer looked down at his phone due to the conversation being abruptly disconnected. "I looked at my phone and I thought, why did you hang up on me because the line was dead and then I began looking around to see my phone lines were dead and the internet was gone and realized we had a major problem." At that point, Stammer ran down to the east end of the Emergency Operations Center that opens to the ground level. He watched the tornado make its way across the south of the city. It was wrapped in rain, making the tornado appear somewhat invisible. At first, they thought it was a rain shape, which is up and down. However, this tornado was wedge-shaped "and a big one." At that point, Stammer had to "find out what had happened to [Joplin]," he states. He and his team started calling people.

Within a given year, Stammer and his team run anywhere from five to nine disaster drills. These include drills for all different sizes and types of disasters, including active shooter, tornado, flood, heat, earthquake, or anything that can cause isolated or widespread catastrophe. In fact, just four days prior to the tornado, the team had participated for four hours in a full-scale national level exercise (spanning seven states in two FEMA regions) for a possible earthquake along the New Madrid Fault from St. Louis down to Memphis.

Stammer explained that, to a large extent, the type of disaster doesn't matter much because the response and recovery are typically the same. Stammer described the standard Incident Command System procedure: "You're going to take care of people first, scene management second, and property preservation last.... So, whether it's a nuclear strike or a tornado or a hazmat situation those are your priorities—one, two and three. We were ripping down buildings and clearing out streets trying to get to the people... This was the Mission."

1. **People** – any human being.
2. **Scene management** – the team.
3. **Property preservation** – if people are needing to be taken care of and property has been destroyed.

An Incident Command System is used to follow the standard Federal Emergency Management Agency guidelines and form Unified Command. Unified Command, instead of having one Incident Commander, is a committee made up of stakeholders including police, fire, ambulance services, public works, the health department, city administrators, state personnel, and any other entity deemed significant in this situation. As a group, they decide the priorities and lead the charge for that section. Stammer stated that this had been practiced many times.

Asked what caught him off guard the most, Stammer's reply was, "the scale of the incident, the size.... We had the 2008 Mother's Day tornado and lost more than a dozen people and two ice storms in 2007.... We had tornadoes in 2003. It's not like we didn't know how to do this and know what was entailed but no one wants to believe it's this bad." He went on to say that "the first real indication of how bad it was, is when I began to get body counts—that was the major indicator for me." After eighteen years in emergency management, Stammer knew this was a full-scale disaster in state and federal response.

"The first few hours in most severe incidents are pandemonium—understanding what happened to you and what you can do about it and then doing your best to marshal. Breaking it out, you have the first 12 hours, first 24, 36, and 72 are the most critical times." The tornado happened on Sunday night, and they found the last deceased person on Tuesday. By this point, search and rescue had made six passes through the city Sunday through Friday on a 24/7 rotation. There were five thousand volunteers representing 435 response agencies. Within a six-month timeframe, the total registered volunteers equaled 175,000.

"With this many volunteers, the key is to get the volunteers into organized groups and have specific missions for them to be the most effective." For those in the Emergency Operations Center, it was critical to process what needed to be done immediately, with three components— people, scene management, and property— as the main guiding factors. The responders on the ground had only one mission—save lives.

"The Freeman Hospital had one-hundred patients in the first fifteen minutes and six-hundred patients in the first hour." Overall deaths were counted at 161, with approximately twelve hundred injuries. Managing 175,000 volunteers was not complicated due to proper planning and experience. The first protocol was using the Emergency Operations Plan. Part of the plan was utilizing resources, such as the American Red Cross and AmeriCorps, to begin the process of registering the volunteers and starting property cleanup. Along with this, "we have a working relationship with our faith-based communities. Most every large faith-based organization has a disaster relief component of which they know each other and travel together to these critical situations." One of these, the Seventh Day Adventist Church, specializing in warehouse management and volunteer registration, came in and set up a Multi-Agency Warehouse (MAW) at Missouri Southern University in Joplin. This became the volunteers' base. Stammer, organized and methodical, drove home the fact that they did not want people to just jump in, haphazardly, and start helping. The problem with a haphazard approach is that it creates a vacuum with everyone wanting to do what they deem is needed, resulting in chaos.

Once the initial search and rescue was complete, the Friday following the aftermath, it was a matter of having the volunteer base and non-response personnel begin clearing the three million cubic yards of debris. Put into context, 9/11 had 600,000 cubic yards of debris, so Joplin had five times more. Thanks to organized and understood missions, the heart of the clean-up was completed in just over two months. The United States Army Corps of Engineers, in conjunction with the state, lead construction contracts, demolition, and removal within Environmental Protection Agency regulations, making cleanup quick and effective.

For the first eleven days, an Incident Report Team worked through each night to publish an Incident Action Plan (IAP) of the previous day's work to be assessed the following day. Listed in the daily IAP were goals and their implementation, needed equipment and its location, a list of communication radio frequencies, the day's schedule (down to porta-potty locations), phone numbers of department heads, and a map of the entire area. The IAP was delivered like clockwork each morning at 7 a.m., giving clear direction to everyone for what needed to be accomplished that day. Once the initial eleven days ended, the IAP process was implemented weekly and later monthly, ending on August 6.

When the mission is clear and the people involved know how their part helps reach the overall goal, there is a greater probability of attainment within a shorter period of time.

Looking back, if Stammer had to do it over again, he said, "The real temptation is to have a drill about something we know about, let's do what we've always done. I think if I had to do it over again, I would have trained for a tornado that was bigger than us. Who imagines you'll be hurt to the point that you can't take care of yourself?" With this message, Stammer encourages other communities to take a map of the disaster area in Joplin, six miles long and three-quarter miles wide, and overlay it on a section of their city to help create better disaster drills for their communities. "Thinking outside the box is a good thing... Yes, this can happen to you and your city," he commonly tells other managers and team members he mentors.

In all, a collaborated, organized, and implemented mission helped Joplin prevail through this difficult time. There were 7,500 structures damaged and another 4,000 destroyed, the majority of those being homes. FEMA was able to bring in 567 mobile housing units to reduce city defection and keep the population in Joplin. Today, Joplin is moving forward by maintaining and growing in population.

As for Stammer, he has given well over 300 lectures within three years, helping other cities, states, and countries prepare for disaster relief in situations such as this.

Joplin's recovery has been remarkable. Today, the city, with rebuilt schools and flourishing industries, stands as a testament to resilience and dedication. For cities and organizations alike, Joplin's story underlines the importance of understanding one's mission, especially in the face of adversity. Joplin has become a beacon of hope and restoration. They are a people of resilience and dedication. In the aftermath of their most disastrous event, they are striving to accomplish their mission to achieve their vision of building a stronger community.

In a critical environment, the mission becomes more of a challenge, but it is extremely important that everyone understands who is in charge and what each individual's part is within the mission. Invariably, people are either leaders or followers. In Joplin's case, no matter who was leading or following, people's safety and accountability was most critical. In every scenario, the people must know what is expected so the mission moves forward and is ultimately accomplished.

The main idea is that, regardless of whether an organization has just one or many missions, they all must be understood. The definition of mission is, once again, a special assignment that is given to a person or group. People need to know their mission, and it must align with achieving the vision.

Mission Overview

The sequence of VMV places the mission critically between vision and values. The mission bridges the gap, each step drawing closer to the vision, while also reinforcing and preserving the organization's core values.

Missions manifest as daily objectives and long-term strategic plans. They answer the pivotal question: How do we achieve the vision? This is accomplished through well-defined missions that are specific, comprehensively outlined, and universally understood. Missions need to be coherent, align with the vision, be tactically designed, and purposeful. They must resonate. If individuals or groups fail to adhere to the mission, they're less likely to succeed. It's crucial for everyone to synchronize with the mission, believing it's the steppingstone for the overarching vision to thrive.

Chipotle's response to the E. coli outbreak serves as a compelling example of a mission-driven pivot. Observing the potential demise of their brand, they swiftly rectified their course, enhancing their protocols on restaurant hygiene. This proactive approach spurred a remarkable recovery from a crisis that could have decimated a reputable company. A mission should be more than just bolstering shareholder value. Prioritizing customers and delivering quality inevitably benefits everyone in the chain, including the shareholders. Aiming for short-term profits by slashing essential procedures isn't the solution. Sometimes, missions might need recalibration, shifting from expansion to recovery, and revisiting the fundamental questions: "who, what, when, where, how, and why." These queries act as the compass for the mission, providing direction, preparing the team for challenges, and maintaining focus on the vision.

Miracles transpire when a mission transforms into a collective conviction. It's at this juncture that the vision grips an organization, penetrating the very souls of its members. The vitality of the vision is sustained by activating and accomplishing these missions. In essence, missions make miracles happen!

Values

Hands-on, value driven—insisting that executives keep in touch with the firm's essential business.

Tom Peters[53]

Values – a person's principles or standards of behavior; one's judgment of what is important in life.[54]

The following is a Code of Ethics letter sent from then-CEO of Enron, Kenneth Lay, to his 20,600 team members on July 1, 2000.

> To: All employees
> From: CEO
> Department: Office of the chairman
> Subject: Code of Ethics
> Date: July 1, 2000
>
> *As officers and employees of Enron Corp, its subsidiaries, and its affiliated companies ("Enron" or collectively the "Company"), we are responsible for conducting the business affairs of the Company in accordance with all applicable laws and in a moral and honest manner. To make certain that we understand what is expected of us, Enron has adopted certain policies, with the approval of the board of directors, all of which are set forth in the enclosed booklet, revised July 2000. Please note that Enron has added the principles of human rights; provided further description of our business ethics policy with respect to our legal contracts, the selection of outside counsel, and the making of disparaging remarks, oral or written, about Enron by employees; provided further*

> *clarification of Enron's policy with respect to confidential information and trade secrets; decreased the number of days passwords are valid under Enron's communication services and equipment policy; provided additional information with respect to the criminal penalties and civil fines assessed by the US government under the Foreign Corrupt Practices Act; and clarified Enron's policy with respect to conflicts of interests, investments and outside business interests of employees. The Code of Ethics contains common sense rules of conduct with which the great majority of Enron employees routinely conform. However, I ask that you read them carefully and completely and that, as you do, you reflect on your past actions to make certain that you have complied with the policies. It is absolutely essential that you fully comply with these policies in the future. If you have any questions, talk them over with your supervisor, manager, or Enron legal counsel.*

Sounds like something we would all aspire for in our values, right? Four months later, we would witness the beginnings of Enron crumbling. On December 2, 2001, Enron filed for bankruptcy due to fraud, deceit, and overall conflicting values.[55]

Values = R.I.C.E.

Enron had these four values on their walls for everyone to see:

- Respect
- Integrity
- Communication
- Excellence

> ***Respect:*** *We treat others as we would like to be treated ourselves. We do not tolerate abusive or disrespectful treatment. Ruthlessness, callousness, and arrogance don't belong here.*

Integrity: *We work with customers and prospects openly, honestly, and sincerely. When we say we will do something, we will do it; when we say we cannot or will not do something, then we won't do it.*

Communication: *We have an obligation to communicate. Here, we take the time to talk with one another and to listen. We believe that the information is meant to move, and that information moves people.*

Excellence: *We are satisfied with nothing less than the very best in everything we do. We will continue to raise the bar for everyone. The great fun here will be for all of us to discover just how good we can really be.*

"Enron stands on the foundation of its Vision and Values. Every employee is educated about the Company's Vision and Values and is expected to conduct business with other employees, partners, contractors, suppliers, vendors, and customers keeping in mind respect, integrity, communication, and excellence. Everything we do evolves from Enron's Vision and Values statements.

"At Enron, we treat others as we expect to be treated ourselves. We believe in respect for the rights of all individuals and are committed to promoting an environment characterized by dignity and mutual respect for employees, customers, contractors, suppliers, partners, community members, and representatives of all levels of Government."

"We are dedicated to conducting business according to all applicable local and international laws and regulations, including, but not limited to, the U.S. Foreign Corrupt Practices Act, and with the highest professional and ethical standards."

"Agreements, whether contractual or verbal, will be honored. No bribes, bonuses, kickbacks, lavish entertainment, or gifts will be given or received in exchange for special position, price, or privilege."

> *"Relations with Enron's many publics – customers, stockholders, governments, employees, suppliers, press and bankers – will be conducted in honesty, candor, and fairness."*
>
> *"Laws and regulations affecting the Company will be obeyed. Even though the laws and business practices of foreign nations may differ from those in effect in the United States, the applicability of both foreign and U.S. laws to the Company's operations will be strictly observed. Illegal behavior on the part of any employee in the performance of Company duties will neither be condoned nor tolerated."*[56]

Why Are Values Important?

The CEO who lies to others in public will eventually start lying to himself in private.

Warren Buffett

Constructing a building requires materials like cement and iron, coupled with precise measurements and dedicated effort, to establish a reliable foundation. Every structure, whether a towering skyscraper or a modest home, should have a foundation designed with the confidence that it can withstand any environmental challenge.

Similarly, the foundation of successful organizations isn't composed of tangible materials but of vision, mission, and values. In the blueprint of a business, these intangible components are as vital as the bricks and mortar in physical constructions.

Values are the core of the core, the heart of the organization - the element that sets a course for prosperity or failure regardless of the state of the organization. Enron lost its way by ignoring the core values it had set for itself, and though the Code of Ethics letter was designed to reintroduce and remind team members of the company's core values, it was too late. Their value system, the foundation of their vision and mission, had been cracked and then destroyed by people who no longer cared for the organization's ethical standards. If an organization's value system isn't upheld from the top down, it diminishes its significance and requires a necessity for stronger leadership.

Enron's team members weren't entirely bad people. They did not set out to destroy the business they had built. However, a series of small lapses in judgment, compounded over time, culminated in grave misdeeds that significantly tarnished the company's reputation. Enron allowed these missteps to dictate their future, and in the end, it dismantled one of the largest companies in the world—all because a core value system was broken.

So, what's the significance of values? They are paramount. If not nurtured and emphasized, their essence can fade, giving rise to disillusionment and mistrust. Enhancing a company doesn't necessarily mean altering its values, but rather elevating their importance consistently. The ideal outcome is that the values resonate not just within the organization but also permeate the lives of its team members and, subsequently, outside the four walls. A robust value system exudes positive influence far and wide.

In the end, every organization's essence is its vision, mission, and values. Among these, values are the fundamental core, holding everything together.

The Simon Sinek Equation:

Values X Behavior = Culture

Values are the cornerstone of any enterprise. In organizations, steadfast values lead to what I like to call "brick wall behavior," meaning it is concrete and determined. A culture steeped in these principles emerges naturally, nurtured by persistent actions and enduring values.

Cultivating a Value-Centered Culture

A value-centered culture originates with a passionate individual. Naturally, people gravitate towards such a beacon of consistency. When bound by a robust value system, a tribe, united by a shared understanding and ambition for success, emerges. But what truly fuels a culture grounded in positive values? It's the collective embrace of shared values, reflected in every facet of the organization—from its inner workings to its external engagements.

In his book, "Tribes," Seth Godin characterizes this collective as individuals discovering unique commonalities. Suppose you're overseas and you encounter a person from the same country—the shared nationality instantly forms a bond, essentially spawning a tribe. Similarly, in the vast expanse of New York City, if you meet someone from your hometown, an instant connection arises. At its heart, values are the bonding agent, forming the foundation upon which tribes endure.[57]

To truly thrive, values must be intricately woven into a tribe's fabric; otherwise, the bond disintegrates rapidly. Consider this: you meet that fellow state resident in New York, but upon deeper conversation, realize you don't align on fundamental values. The bond you believed existed dissolves almost instantly. This scenario echoes what transpires in organizations. When values are compromised or neglected, even the tiniest cracks in the system can widen, causing foundational disintegration. For individuals to navigate the complexities of product quality, service excellence, colleague interaction, and organizational evolution, values are indispensable.

At their essence, core values are the life force of an organization, radiating outward, shaping its subconscious character and culture, which then resonates with consumers. In essence, these values serve as a pivotal structural beam, supporting both the organization's framework and its broader mission.

Company Values

Paradigm Shift

Paradigm Shift: Pioneering Change Amidst Crisis

Paradigm Shift stands out as one of America's rapidly expanding professional development firms. Catering to organizational levels ranging from executives to frontline leaders, they also have a significant footprint in nationwide educational initiatives. Their hallmark offerings included a blend of camps and after-school programs, collaborating with notable endeavors like Upward Bound, Trio, and Gear UP programs.

Jerrod Murr, the company's founder and Chief Visionary Officer, embodies resilience. His leadership style is steeped in inspiration, consistently championing Paradigm Shift's seven foundational values. When the COVID-19 pandemic disrupted the norm, Murr's agility came to the fore. With multiple client engagements on hold or canceled, Murr and his team plunged into devising innovative and uplifting strategies to bolster the morale and growth of their clients' teams and fortify educational sectors.

The unprecedented challenges of 2020 were discerned by Paradigm Shift as an influential moment. Aggressively, they shifted gears towards crafting solutions that would steer teenagers and educational personnel from apathy due to prolonged school shutdowns to overcoming hurdles. One standout initiative was 'Engage 2020', which featured Adventure Kits designed for both digital and traditional usage. This period saw Paradigm Shift's core values being put through their paces, culminating in a renewed commitment to community welfare. Their proactive measures fortified thousands of educators, students, and administrative staff across their educational partnerships. In parallel, they also amplified professional growth for their corporate partners. By the close of 2020, Paradigm Shift's impressive track record encompassed training over 1,400 professionals and facilitators via video conferencing, underscoring their business's exponential growth in challenging times.

Paradigm Shift Core Values

EXPECT GREATNESS *- the refractor telescope*

We must look beyond what we can see with the naked eye. All too often, we limit ourselves to what we see right in front of us. Our failures. Our weaknesses. Our doubts. With this view, we limit the God-given ability within each of us. We are capable of far more than we assume. At Paradigm Shift, we change the expectation. We do not move with arrogance toward inevitable success, but rather, we march with confidence toward the opportunities that lie before us. Be Your Best. Dream. Expect Greatness.

PICK UP CHAIRS *- the metal folding chair*

We do what needs to be done when it needs to be done. This isn't always glamorous, but that's leadership. True leaders are not looking to be served, but to serve. We do not strive to be first, but rather are the first to strive. Leadership at Paradigm Shift is not about receiving credit, gaining game or pandering to praise. Servanthood is leadership. Work Hard. Serve Others. Pick Up Chairs.

FIERCELY INCLUSIVE *- the footbridge*

An invitation may be the single most powerful act we possess as humans. It is when we invite people into our world, that our world can begin to grow. We work to include people who think, act, and believe differently than we do so we can learn and grow. It is our goal to unite, not divide. Division is easy. It is the hard work of inclusion, the messiness of community, that will bring about real change in this world. Honestly Care. Love Much. Be Fiercely Inclusive.

STAY ABOVE REPROACH *- the human heart*

We must guard our hearts. Good intentions are not enough. The human heart is deceitful above all things. Who can understand it? This is about integrity. Our words and intentions must align with our actions. We do not lie, cheat, or cut corners. We do not put ourselves or others in questionable situations. We do not compromise our beliefs. We do not apologize for our values. Guard Your Heart. Help Others. Stay Above Reproach.

DO HARD THINGS - *the round point shovel*

Difficulty is a relative term. What may be overwhelming for some is simple for others. The commonality between us all, however, is the aversion to difficult tasks. Most humanity has accepted this fate as final. The world is full of people who will settle. We will not be such people. We will consistently stretch ourselves to do things that are out of our comfort zone or just beyond our abilities. It may be hard but that will not stop us. Work Hard. Stretch. Do Hard Things.

HAVE FUN - *the wooden yo-yo*

Life is entirely too short not to enjoy it. We will spend much of our waking adult hours at work. Going to work should be a joy, not a chore. At Paradigm Shift, we choose to have fun. We recognize the power of perception. Everyday tasks can be viewed with excitement. Coworkers can be dear friends. Work can be an adventure. We choose the adventure. Enjoy Life. Play. Have Fun.

MOVE MOUNTAINS - *the hot air balloon*

Mountains come in all shapes and sizes. It is not our place to judge someone's obstacles, but to help them progress, to move forward. The journey is long. We will move mountains for ourselves and others. If there is a challenge in front of us, we will not ignore it, we will face it. All too often, we settle for the obstructed view before us when our dream, our goal, our hope is waiting just over the mountaintop. Think Bigger. Never Settle. Move Mountains.[58]

Dunkin' Donuts

The mission statement of Dunkin' Donuts and Dunkin' Brands:

The original mission statement (referred to as the "philosophy") of Dunkin' Donuts came straight from the founder, William Rosenburg:

> *"Make and serve the freshest, most delicious coffee and donuts quickly and courteously in modern, well merchandised stores."*

The parent company of Dunkin' Donuts franchise, Dunkin' Brands has twelve seven values and five principles that the company believes should guide the decisions of everyone associated with Baskin-Robbins retail outlets (Dunkin' Donuts' sister company) and lead all Dunkin' Donuts franchisees to success. The Dunkin' Brands Values and Guiding Principles are:

"Our Values"

- Honesty - Embrace the truth about oneself and the world.
- Transparency - Demonstrate openness and vulnerability.
- Humility - Acknowledge your own mistakes and commit to learning.
- Integrity - Say what you think and do what you say.
- Respectfulness - Honor the dignity, inclusion, and diversity of others.
- Fairness - Do what is right based on common principles.
- Responsibility - Make yourself accountable to the community.

"Our Guiding Principles"

- Leadership - Responsibility with passion at every level.
- Innovation - Excellence in everything we do.
- Execution - Ownership and accountability for results, success, and failure.
- Social Stewardship - Demonstration of good corporate citizenship and responsibility to all constituencies.

- Fun - Approach every challenge with enthusiasm, energy, and excitement... celebrate every step of the way!

Dunkin' Donuts is one of the more aggressive companies when writing about vision, mission, and values. If you'll notice the principles are the deeper descriptions of the values.[59]

Disney

Disney's Core Values:

- Make everyone's dreams come true, you better believe it
- Never a customer, always a guest
- All for one and one for all
- Share the spotlight
- Dare to dare
- Practice, practice, practice
- Make your elephant fly
- Capture the magic with storyboards.

Disney's approach to personalizing their core values is truly commendable. While unique to Disney, the values resonate universally. Disney continues to enhance and "plus" as Walt Disney himself made note.[60]

"You can design and create and build the most wonderful place in the world, but it takes people to make the dream a reality." Walt Disney[61]

With or Without Specific Core Values

Subway

In the journals of successful corporations, there's often a compelling genesis. Subway, for instance, was born out of a desire for higher education. Fred DeLuca sought to fund his medical school tuition and, in 1965, pitched an idea to a friend, Peter Buck. Buck proposed the concept of a sandwich shop with "submarine" as part of its branding. Thus, "Pete's Super Submarines" was born in Bridgeport, Connecticut. The name would evolve to "Subway" by 1968.

Starting with a modest investment of $1,000 (equivalent to $7,500 today), Subway's trajectory was upward. By 1981, it boasted 200 franchises. In just a year, that figure surged to 300. Today, Subway stands as the largest restaurant chain globally, with over 44,000 outlets. Yet, how could a behemoth with such an inspiring origin stumble in terms of mission and values?

Subway's trajectory took an unexpected turn in 2015.

A Turn of Events

The backstory – the year 2000 when a certain Jared Scot Fogle caught attention. A feature in Men's Health titled "Stupid Diets... that Work!" chronicled Fogle's 245-pound weight loss journey attributed to his self-styled "Subway Diet." This feature, noticed by a Chicago Subway franchisee and later relayed to an advertising agency, catapulted Jared to fame. Jared's endorsement, coupled with the introduction of the $5 footlong campaign in 2008, sent Subway's sales through the roof.[62]

However, relying heavily on an external individual as the embodiment of a brand carries inherent risks. For Subway, the seemingly unassuming Jared had a concealed, sinister side. In August 2015, he pleaded guilty to charges related to child exploitation and received a prison sentence of five years.

Subway's ordeal stresses the perils of aligning a brand too closely with a personality without comprehensive vetting. What's interesting is to see how such a massive organization can use a person to represent its brand without ensuring the face of the brand is in sync with its core values. To put it into perspective, it happens every day with team members who carry the torch of any company. This should encourage organizations everywhere to enforce more transparency of their values. All team members, from every facet, are extensions of the brand.[63]

Subway's Mission Statements:

While Subway's current mission statement appears robust, my research didn't identify any explicit core values within the corporation. Instead, the mission statement often surfaced when searching for specific core values.

In 2011, Subway's mission statement read: *"To delight every customer so they want to tell their friends—offering great value through fresh, delicious, made-to-order sandwiches and an exceptional experience."*

This mission appears to have steered the brand effectively, seeing as Subway expands from a singular store in 1965 to almost 40,000 outlets globally by the end of this period.

By 2013, their mission evolved to: *"To provide the tools and knowledge enabling entrepreneurs to successfully compete in the global Fast-Food industry, consistently offering value to consumers with great tasting food that's beneficial for them and crafted to their preferences."*

This shift over the years indicates Subway's adaptability and emphasis on consumer preference and empowerment of its franchisees. Still, a more explicit outline of core values would further strengthen their brand identity and direction.

The Integral Role of Core Values

Core values guide the everyday actions of each individual within an organization, forming the bedrock upon which the mission and vision of the business are achieved. They shape the company's characteristics and are maintained in customer interactions, experiences -- vibe, and the priorities set by leadership.

In the case of Subway, there isn't a clearly defined set of core values that articulates the internal operations of the company. However, their 2011 mission statement aimed to "Delight every customer so they want to tell their friends." This statement paints a vivid picture. If a customer is eager to share their Subway experience with friends, it implies a notably positive interaction.

Such a mission permeates the work of every Subway Sandwich Artist. If these sandwich makers truly grasp the mission to delight every customer, they'll endeavor to offer more than just a sandwich: they will provide a delectable, high-quality, wholesome meal paired with a warm and inviting customer experience. Such admirable service acts as a magnet. It not only encourages customers to return but also achieves the mission's intent — compelling customers to spread the word about their delightful Subway visit.

It's a given that every team member of a company, including its external associates, must echo the organization's values. The extensions (e.g., shipping, receiving, customer service, fulfillment as a whole), if contracted, should hold the same value system, or the weak link will quickly surface, and customers defect without fail. This happens too often, and in some cases, it's too late to place the gauze over the wound in an effort to decrease and ultimately stop any hemorrhaging.

It's essential to clarify that the absence of clearly listed core values doesn't imply a company is poorly run or employs people lacking in integrity. There can be outliers in any organization that simply don't align with its values. However, it's pivotal to have an established set of core values that serves as the organizations playbook for growth and character development. Core values arm leadership with the tools to guide from within, nurturing a cohesive and dedicated team.

OfficeMax

Take OfficeMax's core values. In 2013, OfficeMax was acquired by Office Depot. However, OfficeMax's core values were so strong that most people in leadership positions were handed the leadership playbook having the five core values listed with explanations defining each core value.

OfficeMax's Core Values:

1. Uphold Integrity and Accountability
2. Prioritize Both Company and Customer Interests
3. Embrace Teamwork Rooted in Trust
4. Consistently Focus and Exhibit Discipline
5. Foster a Sense of Urgency[64]

These core values streamline decision-making within the organization. When interacting with customers, team members can simply reflect, "Is this action beneficial for both the company and the customer?" And when internal disputes arise, leadership can evaluate: "Is this a breach of our 'Teamwork Rooted in Trust'? Does it align with 'Uphold Integrity and Accountability'?" These values serve as a leadership playbook for the entire organization.

As Tom Peters insightfully points out in his book *In Search of Excellence*, "Brutal consistency breeds success." Every organization must prioritize its vision, mission, and values.

The "Rank and Yank" Methodology

In the absence of core values, team members lack a foundational framework to guide their decisions and set personal objectives. Enron's operational methodologies, seemingly effective initially, sowed the seeds of its downfall. When values center solely on metrics like "maximizing shareholder value" or "success at any cost", it skews the very essence of an organization's genuine value proposition.

Enron's CEO, Jeffrey Skilling, championed the "rank and yank" approach, ranking sales team members by their performance metrics. The bottom 15 percent faced potential layoffs. Although such a strategy could momentarily motivate some to perform better, its long-term impact was damaging. When performance pressures mounted, team members resorted to dishonesty to project an illusion of success.

Real success stems from dedication, intellect, and obsessive focus. But in challenging business climates, or during downturns, enforcing stringent performance metrics can foster negative behaviors. In Enron's scenario, instead of fostering genuine dedication and innovation, it nurtured unethical practices which ultimately polluted not just Enron but its business associates.

Behavior sets the tone for an organization. Once entrenched, it replicates and amplifies, much like the embedding of core values. Both leadership and staff must exude behaviors that align with positive core values. As Simon Sinek aptly puts it, *"Values x Behavior = Culture."*

Enron's regular "rank and yank" evaluations escalated competition to an unhealthy level, cultivating a culture riddled with deception. This, combined with other internal malpractices, culminated in Enron's spectacular downfall.

Contrastingly, Berkshire Hathaway, a multifaceted conglomerate with a legacy dating back to 1839 and assets nearing $1 trillion as of 2022, stands as a testament to ethical business practices. Spearheaded by Warren Buffett since 1964, it evolved from its textile roots to a mammoth conglomerate. Buffett's annual letters to shareholders encapsulate the company's integrity, highlighting its ventures and spotlighting avenues for sustainable growth.

Buffett's 1978 Letter To Shareholders:

Paragraph #1: *... A second complication arising from the merger is that the 1977 figures shown in this report are different from the 1977 figures shown in the report we mailed to you last year. Accounting convention requires that when two entities such as Diversified and Berkshire are merged, all financial data subsequently must be presented as if the companies had been merged at the time they were formed rather than just recently. So the enclosed financial statements, in effect, pretend that in 1977 (and earlier years) the Diversified-Berkshire merger already had taken place, even though the actual merger date was December 30, 1978. This shifting base makes comparative commentary confusing and, from time to time in our narrative report, we will talk of figures and performance for Berkshire shareholders as historically reported to you rather than as restated after the Diversified merger.*

Paragraph #2: *With that preamble it can be stated that, with or without restated figures, 1978 was a good year. Operating earnings, exclusive of capital gains, at 19.4% of beginning shareholders' investment were within a fraction of our 1972 record. While we believe it is improper to include capital gains or losses in evaluating the performance of a single year, they are an important component of the longer-term record. Because of such gains, Berkshire's long-term growth in equity per share has been greater than would be indicated by compounding the returns from operating earnings that we have reported annually.*

Paragraph #3: *For example, over the last three years - generally a bonanza period for the insurance industry, our largest profit producer - Berkshire's per share net worth virtually has doubled, thereby compounding at about 25% annually through a combination of good operating earnings and fairly substantial capital gains. Neither this 25% equity gain from all sources, nor the 19.4% equity gain from operating earnings in 1978 is sustainable. The insurance cycle has turned downward in 1979, and it is almost certain that operating earnings measured by return on equity will fall this year. However, operating earnings measured in dollars are likely to increase on the much larger shareholders' equity now employed in the business.*

Paragraph #4: *In contrast to this cautious view about near term return from operations, we are optimistic about prospects for long term return from major equity investments held by our insurance companies. We make no attempt to predict how security markets will behave; successfully forecasting short term stock price movements is something we think neither we nor anyone else can do. In the longer run, however, we feel that many of our major equity holdings are going to be worth considerably more money than we paid, and that investment gains will add significantly to the operating returns of the insurance group.*

In 1978, Buffett's letter to Berkshire Hathaway stockholders championed transparency and candor. Without hedging or evading, he presented the facts as they were. This forthrightness not only solidified the trust and support of his shareholders but also set the stage for the significant and nearly inevitable growth that Berkshire Hathaway would experience under his leadership.

Paragraph #1 describes the complications to the merger that took place and the expectations of such a merger.

Paragraph #2 states, *"While we believe it is improper to include capital gains or losses in evaluating the performance of a single year, they are an important component of the longer-term record."* This statement shows consistency in integrity from the foundation up and allows for possible flaws and an understanding of the potential pitfalls of future development.

Paragraph # 3 states, *"Neither this 25% equity gain from all sources, nor the 19.4% equity gain from operating earnings in 1978 is sustainable. The insurance cycle has turned downward in 1979, and it is almost certain that operating earnings measured by return on equity will fall this year."*

This passage portrays a company that sparks enthusiasm—a place where individuals are eager to work, seeing their roles not just as jobs but as investments in future rewards. It doesn't promise consistently high dividends; rather, it establishes a foundation for all stakeholders, from team members to investors, to anticipate sustained growth over the long term. Through this narrative, stakeholders gain a more lucid insight into the company's direction, mission, and vision for the years ahead.

Paragraph #4: After the introductory three paragraphs, this section rolls out the red carpet, inviting readers to explore the exciting potential and opportunities that lie ahead for the company. *"We make no attempt to predict how security markets will behave; successfully forecasting short term stock price movements are something we think neither we nor anyone else can do."*[65]

Fast forward: Buffett's 2013 letter to shareholders

Further gains in float will be tough to achieve. On the plus side, GEICO's float will almost certainly grow. In National Indemnity's reinsurance division, however, we have a number of run-off contracts whose float drifts downward. If we do experience a decline in float at some future time, it will be very gradual – at the outside no more than 3% in any year. The nature of our insurance contracts is such that we can never be subject to immediate demands for sums that are large compared to our cash resources. (In this respect, property-casualty insurance differs in an important way from certain forms of life insurance.)

If our premiums exceed the total of our expenses and eventual losses, we register an underwriting profit that adds to the investment income our float produces. When such a profit is earned, we enjoy the use of free money – and, better yet, get paid for holding it.

Unfortunately, the wish of all insurers to achieve this happy result creates intense competition, so vigorous in most years that it causes the P/C industry as a whole to operate at a significant underwriting loss. This loss, in effect, is what the industry pays to hold its float. For example, State Farm, by far the country's largest insurer and a well-managed company besides, incurred an underwriting loss in nine of the twelve years ending in 2012 (the latest year for which their financials are available, as I write this).

Competitive dynamics almost guarantee that the insurance industry – despite the float income all companies enjoy – will continue its dismal record of earning subnormal returns as compared to other businesses.

In a year in which most equity managers found it impossible to outperform the S&P 500, both Todd Combs and Ted Weschler handily did so. Each now runs a portfolio exceeding $7 billion. They've earned it.

I must again confess that their investments outperformed mine. (Charlie says I should add "by a lot.") If such humiliating comparisons continue, I'll have no choice but to cease talking about them.

Todd and Ted have also created significant value for you in several matters unrelated to their portfolio activities. Their contributions are just beginning: Both men have Berkshire blood in their veins.[66]

The 2013 letter to shareholders clearly lays out the potential gains and losses of Berkshire Hathaway. Buffett's shareholder letters from both 1978 and 2013 share a common thread: they are candid, forthright, and genuine. While society may find this to be remarkable, it is actually quite unremarkable. Buffet conditioned his shareholders with unremarkable context year-over-year, therefore creating a remarkably trusted brand.

While expectations can breed disappointment, Buffet has become a consistent messenger who delivers expected, repeatable outcomes. Consistent messaging with integrity and accountability at the core of its value systems creates a business climate society wants to participate and be part of.

We want to be a part of something clear, with a vision—
to believe in something transparent and truthful.

There's an innate human desire to be associated with clarity and a discernible vision—to put faith in something genuine and transparent. Warren Buffett has brilliantly embodied this with Berkshire Hathaway. At the conclusion of the 2013 letter, notably in *"Paragraph #3"*, Buffett showcases authentic leadership by highlighting the achievements of Todd Combs and Ted Weschler. Recognizing and celebrating the contributions of others is a testament to true leadership. And who wouldn't want to passionately contribute to such a cause? It's this kind of vision and values that draws people in, motivating them to align with the organization's mission.

There is a massive contrast between how Berkshire Hathaway and Enron conducted business. The results speak for themselves and show the true, organic nature of how vision, mission, and values drive incredible outcomes or lead it down a path of catastrophic failure.

Coach Wooden - 1st Practice

John Wooden, born in 1910 in the Hoosier state of Indiana, carved a remarkable path in the world of basketball. Standing at 5' 10", a 17-year-old Wooden led his Martinsville High School basketball team to the state championship in 1927. His prowess on the court continued at Purdue University, where he played as a guard and clinched three MVP titles.

After graduating in 1934 with an English degree, Wooden combined his passion for teaching and sports. He taught English at Dayton High School in Dayton, Kentucky, and coached baseball, tennis, and basketball. It was during this phase of life that he began to sculpt his leadership philosophy, the *"Pyramid of Success."* Aimed at instilling values in his students and players, these principles would later become a hallmark of his tenure as head coach at UCLA.

The Pyramid of Success encompasses principles like enthusiasm, cooperation, loyalty, friendship, industriousness, intentness, initiative, alertness, self-control, team spirit, skill, condition, confidence, poise, and competitive greatness, all underpinned by faith and patience.

Wooden's coaching style was both iconic and understated. He was known for his poise and his genuine desire to see his players thrive, both on the court and in life. Among his many accolades, he is celebrated for steering the UCLA team to an unmatched record in 1971 with 88 consecutive wins and just a single loss. Interestingly, that sole defeat was at the hands of Notre Dame. However, in a riveting comeback a week later, UCLA bested Notre Dame 94-75 in Westwood, California, reclaiming their No. 1 spot.

The Wooden Way: Prioritizing Safety

On the first day of practice, Coach Wooden had a peculiar focus: teaching his players to tie their shoes correctly. As he meticulously threaded each lace, starting from the bottom and working upwards, he emphasized the importance of foot care. As he pulled the laces gently through each set of holes, Wooden would talk about why taking care of one's feet was vital to the success of each game.

Bill Walton, a standout player for Wooden in 1971, recounted this unorthodox first day. The entire team, comprised of carefully selected star athletes, spent the entire session mastering the art of shoe-tying. It wasn't just a quick lesson; it was a deliberate practice, reinforcing the significance of a perfect fit.

Most would dismiss shoe-tying as mundane, but Wooden transformed it into an unforgettable *"experience."* This simple exercise conveyed his deep care for every player, highlighting the importance of meticulousness in every task. His intent was clear: correct foot care would enhance the players' running, pivoting, and side-to-side movements.

As Wooden often said, "While a team must excel in countless areas, the overarching vision is paramount." This emphasis on the "minor" act of shoe-tying was indicative of Wooden's commitment to detail. Over his twelve-year tenure as head coach, his unyielding focus on the small details translated into ten national titles.

Wooden wasn't driven by a need for universal approval. He prioritized safety and attention to detail, embodying his core values. And the outcome? Multiple national championships.

Why do some entities, like Enron, mistakenly think they can sidestep the chaos they've created? More often than not, unchecked ego drives flawed leadership. When such arrogance permeates the leadership layer, it jeopardizes the organization's mission, vision, and values. The result is a gradual, then rampant, decline into dishonesty, rendering the company's original foundation unrecognizable.

In Simon Sinek's book *Start with Why*, he explains that fostering a sense of safety among peers is a key mechanism for obtaining satisfaction. This safety extends to team members, teammates, clients, and associates, all desire a secure environment for business interactions. Ensuring such safety fosters long-standing partnerships, whether one's role is that of a customer, vendor, or team member.

The dividends of such a safe and value-centric environment are evident. When core values permeate an organization and shape every action, success is not just possible — it's boundless.[67]

Values In Leadership

The quality of a leader is reflected
in the standards they set for themselves.

Ray Kroc

An organization's values profoundly shape its leadership, the quality of work within that leadership, and the ethos that permeates every individual involved. These values act as foundational pillars, grounding the company's actions and culture. By continuously emphasizing these values and understanding the "why" behind them, an organization can develop a kind of muscle memory, ensuring positive reinforcement flows from the leadership to every level.

In 2015, Volkswagen's scandal, involving the manipulation of emissions systems in 11.5 million vehicles worldwide, came to light. Despite the discovery happening in 2015, the issue traces its origins to 2006. During this time, senior management overruled team member concerns, focusing solely on the turbocharged direct injection (TDI) engine. Engineers, despite recognizing potential issues, felt too intimidated to raise alarms. The "solution" they were coerced into implementing involved a device providing false emissions data. While many were aware of this unethical strategy, a climate of fear and intimidation meant that nobody spoke out. This wasn't merely a team member error; it was a catastrophic leadership failure characterized by a lack of transparency and truth.[68]

The engineers at Volkswagen were undoubtedly talented. Yet, when an environment stifles genuine concerns, due to intimidation, the inevitable downfall begins. The result was a substantial blow to Volkswagen's reputation. A deviation from core values allows deception to seep in, with leadership drifting away from what should be their guiding principles. Just as a rudder steers a ship, values steer an organization and the overarching mission and vision it stands for.

Many perceived Enron's CEO, Kenneth Lay, as an upstanding individual, reinforced by President George W. Bush's endorsement of Lay's charitable efforts - he was a "good guy." Yet, as Adam Grant highlights in his book, *Give and Take*, "although Lay may have looked like a giver to many observers, he was a faker; a taker in disguise."

It's no wonder that people within Enron felt they were given a right to act without accountability. Their actions were based on cues from leadership. As upper management used company funds as if they were their own and manipulated everyone outside Enron's four walls, other team members watched and eventually duplication began. In any organization, once the infection of poor values begins to form within leadership, it's difficult to heal the wound.

Mimi Swartz, in her New York Times op-ed, captured the essence of Lay's character, citing the insights of former executive Mike Muckleroy. Lay's tendency to bend the truth, especially under duress, his impatience, and his deliberate omission of unpleasant realities, painted a picture aligning more with the prosecution's portrayal than the philanthropic image he publicly projected.[69]

It's evident that a clear vision anchored in values wins. The synergy between vision, mission, and values is undeniable. When organizations prioritize and embody their values, they are better equipped to navigate challenges, foster genuine connections, and ultimately achieve enduring success.

Vision, Mission, and Values: The Core Framework

Vision, mission, and values (VMV) serve as the foundational pillars of any organization, group, or team. The vision acts as the guiding beacon, the mission translates this vision into actionable steps, and the values are deeply embedded within the very essence of the individuals.

Consider this framework as the hub of a wheel. The hub encompasses the essential tools, fundamentals, and foundations. If the hub is absent, an organization risks disintegration. In the context of Open-Ended Logic, the wheel hub represents the central point, crucial for sustaining the load and effectively responding to challenges. Just as the hub supports a bicycle's entire weight, transferring energy through the spokes - then rim, beginning the process of movement towards its destination, VMV acts as the core of any entity, whether it's a group, team, or organization. An organization's strength and growth are channeled through its VMV, permeating every facet of its structure and culture.

Without a vision, people perish – direction is lost. Missions align and guide, while values create a steadfast foundation. Together, these elements form a robust core, underpinning an organization's might. The vision lights the way, the mission actualizes the vision, and values provide the endurance needed to overcome challenges, serving as a moral anchor.

As we transition into Part 2 (Structure/The Spokes) and Part 3 (Culture/The Rim), the significance of this core becomes even more pronounced. Walt Disney's meticulous attention to detail is legendary. Just as his team often determined their direction based on Disney's subtle cues, shouldn't VMV, given their centrality, be highlighted more? From the ground level to the upper echelons of leadership, every individual should intimately understand the Vision, Mission, and Values. It's this understanding that truly unlocks an organization's potential.

It's essential not just to establish VMV, but to continuously emphasize, teach, and embody them religiously across all levels of an organization. This ensures that every member is not only aware but truly aligned with the organization's true north. Can we survive without Vision, Mission, and Values? Biblically, we perish without a Vision and that is true, yet we can survive momentarily with the absence of a Vision, Mission, and Values. However, it's virtually impossible to thrive and witness the full potential of anything we do, organizationally, professionally, and personally without them.

We can survive with the absence of Vision, Mission, and Values, but it's virtually impossible to thrive to the fullest without.

Kevin Ragsdale

PART 2: STRUCTURE / THE SPOKES

PARANOIA

THINK

CURIOSITY

PREDICTABLE OUTCOMES

MARGINAL GAINS

SALES

INTELLIGENT DISOBEDIENCE

PREPARATION

Exquisitely Disruptive

Around here... we don't look backwards very long. We keep moving forward, opening up new doors and doing new things.

Walt Disney

Disruption *(noun)* – forcible separation or division into parts (dictionary.com)

Disrupt *(verb; business term)* – to radically change (an industry, business strategy, etc.) as by introducing a new product or service that creates a new market (dictionary.com)

Embracing Disruption: The Double-Edged Sword

Disruption can describe personal changes, new ventures, opening new markets, pushing for change in how business is conducted with customers, or offering more value through exchanges. Disruption is a constant in our world yet is perceived differently when brought in the doors of an organization. From the first automobile to the integrated circuit, markets have been built overnight out of disruptions. With disruption, nations have experienced massive growth and economic acceleration, while also facing great defeat and health-related havoc.

The disruption desired should be aligned with the core— vision, mission, and values, otherwise the organization will inevitably move further from its goal. Embracing disruption from an external perspective is commendable. We champion and herald innovators and disruptors for the advancements they bring. But, when faced with potential disruption in our own domain, it often appears as a looming storm cloud, threatening to upend what we've known and mastered. This thought process is at the heart of disruption's nature: it's a heralded force when we're leading the charge but can seem daunting when we're the ones facing its transformative might.

In the landscape of commerce and innovation, disruption acts as both a beacon of opportunity and a harbinger of challenges. As we navigate this intricate maze, the key is not merely to react but to anticipate, aligning our foundational beliefs with the winds of change. This ensures that we're not just affected by disruption but actively shape it to forge paths that were previously unseen.

Paranoia

Success breeds complacency.
Complacency breeds failure.
Only the paranoid survive.

Andy Groves (Intel CEO)

In the realm of business, the term 'paranoia' might initially raise eyebrows, especially since dictionary.com defines it as "baseless or excessive suspicion of the motives of others." Yet, Andy Groves' advice, "Be paranoid," seems crucial, like stopping at red lights. This brand of business paranoia encapsulates understanding one's identity and mission while continually innovating and progressing, challenging the status quo when it becomes obsolete. It's this mindset that propels Amazon to always operate with a "day-one" philosophy.

When questioned about what "day-two" might look like for Amazon, Bezos remarked that it would signify the company's demise - a pretty alarming statement to say the least. The imperative nature of paranoia becomes evident in tales of organizations that rested on their laurels. When firms adopted a day-two, -three, or -four attitude, they soon recognized that nothing lasts forever, especially customer loyalty. Consumers buy with purpose, share experiences, and undeniably possess a multitude of options.

While loyal customers might await their favored brand's next innovation, we're an impatient bunch. If a rival presents a more appealing proposition, loyalty can quickly waver. Instead of waiting for things to break, why not be the innovator, the door-opener, constantly enhancing services and products? The adage "If it ain't broke, don't fix it," might sound wise, but consider the perspectives of companies like Trans World Airlines, Borders, or Abercrombie & Fitch. Their hindsight might suggest self-disruption, adopting different strategies, and avoiding a complacent, or "day-two" mentality.[70]

Blockbuster & Netflix: A Tale of Disruption

Companies either lead with proactive disruptions or find themselves on the receiving end of external disruptions. Blockbuster was, unfortunately, a recipient of the latter. To comprehend Blockbuster's demise, one must first understand their success.

Amongst an ocean of local video shops, David Cook established the first Blockbuster store on October 19, 1985. By 2004, Blockbuster had expanded to a staggering 9,094 outlets with a workforce of 83,000. Cook's venture exploded onto the scene, making each store a sought-after destination. Blockbuster's stores showcased VHS tapes, and later DVDs, neatly categorized for ease of selection. The stores were designed to be family-friendly and Cook introduced a sophisticated scanning system that was innovative for its time.[71]

In 2000, a pivotal moment in video rental history took place. Reed Hastings, the founder of Netflix, approached Blockbuster proposing a potential partnership. (At the time, Netflix annual revenue was just shy of $36m.) Blockbuster's Dallas corporate team rejected the offer. Hastings, undeterred, pushed forward.

By 2005, Netflix boasted 4.5 million subscribers ($682m rev.), which surged to 16 million by 2010 ($2.16b rev.). Disruption can manifest in various forms. In hindsight, Blockbuster's refusal of an alliance with a budding entrepreneur like Hastings was a monumental misstep.[72,73]

Hastings, having previously sold his company Pure Software for $750 million in 1995, had a track record of success. As Netflix's popularity soared, Blockbuster's stronghold dwindled. Hastings foresaw the transition from physical videos to digital streaming. If Blockbuster had harbored a touch of forward-thinking paranoia, their story might have been different.

Wayne Gretzky's famous words resonate here: "Skate to where the puck is going to be, not where it has been." Initially, Netflix's business model involved shipping DVDs to customers who would then return them. While this didn't immediately alarm Blockbuster, Netflix's consistent growth soon caught their attention.

In a staggering turn of events in 2000, Hastings proposed selling 49 percent of Netflix to Blockbuster to serve as its online wing. Blockbuster declined the $50 million offer. Today, Netflix boasts a valuation of $186 billion. The narrative of Blockbuster and Netflix mirrors the David vs. Goliath parable. If Blockbuster had exhibited agility and a willingness to evolve, perhaps they would be the dominant force in today's world of entertainment.

The Fall of Nokia: Missing the Signs

In 2007, Nokia was a technological behemoth with a valuation of $50 billion. Yet, a mere six years later, the company would be acquired by Microsoft for a fraction of that amount, $7 billion. So, what transpired during this time that diminished Nokia's prominence in the tech world?

Founded in Finland in 1865, Nokia had solidified its status as a technological titan and a Fortune 500 powerhouse. The name Nokia was synonymous with cutting-edge communication. At its zenith, the company claimed over 50 percent of the global cell phone market share. Its dedication to robust hardware and innovative design made it the go-to choice for millions. However, tech, in general, shifted when Apple, led by Steve Jobs, unveiled the iPhone, soon followed by Samsung with its Galaxy series. By 2007, Nokia's position as a tech frontrunner began to fade.

Jobs was not just a visionary or futurist, but a strategist to boot. He understood the lifecycle of cell phones and anticipated users upgrading their devices every couple of years. Unlike the era of the flip phone, where phones were chiefly marketed and distributed through carriers, Jobs imagined a new paradigm. He foresaw smartphones becoming indispensable tools, transcending mere call and text functionalities. To stay competitive, phone manufacturers had to continually innovate. Jobs positioned Apple at the forefront of this shift.

While competitors balked at the iPhone's $600 price tag, Jobs focused on the unparalleled user experience it offered. His vision was to make Apple the benchmark in every product category they entered, be it with the Mac, iPod, or iPhone.

Nokia and Motorola, meanwhile, found themselves trapped in complacency. They misjudged the market - the future, underestimating the consumer's appetite for innovation and adaptability. In contrast, Apple tapped into this hunger, offering futuristic solutions that changed the game.

Such narratives spotlight the dangers that large, seemingly invincible companies face. The very factors that propel them to greatness can also make them vulnerable to irrelevancy. While Nokia prided itself on its text messaging prowess, Apple was redefining multimedia communication.

In a twist of irony, five years before its decline, Nokia engineers had pitched a smartphone concept. However, it was dismissed by the leadership, who believed in the tactile satisfaction of physical buttons and doubted the potential of a smartphone to rival the then-popular BlackBerry. The rest, as they say, is history.[74]

Kmart: From Retail Giant to Irrelevance

Comedian Nate Bargatze humorously captured Kmart's decline in his routine. He recalls wandering into a dimly lit Kmart and jestingly inquiring if the establishment was still operational. He then muses that perhaps customers frequented Kmart to procure shelves for launching their own business. While said in humor, this observation wasn't far from the reality many experienced when visiting a Kmart during its final years—it often felt more like a disorganized flea market than a prominent retail chain.[75]

Kmart, famously known for introducing the "Blue Light Special" in 1969, first opened its doors in 1962. It was an extension of The Kresge Company, which had been in operation since 1899. By the early 1990s, Kmart was a powerhouse with over 2,000 outlets. The company's expansion strategy involved acquiring numerous brands like Office Max, Sports Authority, Walden Book Company, Builders Square, Sears, and more. Alongside these acquisitions, Kmart was known for its innovative training programs, robust marketing strategies, and pioneering celebrity endorsements, having collaborated with stars such as Martha Stewart, Rosie O'Donnell, Adam Levine, and Jaclyn Smith. Technologically, Kmart was a trailblazer, surpassing even Walmart. By the late '70s and '80s, it rose to be the second largest retailer, outpaced only by Sears.

Yet, where did it all go wrong?

Amid its expansive acquisitions and ventures, Kmart lost touch with its core. The brand that once resonated with countless households became increasingly unfamiliar, gradually alienating its loyal customer base. By the time this realization dawned upon Kmart's leadership, Walmart had firmly established its dominance. Although Kmart made attempts to recalibrate and regain its lost clientele, the endeavors were too late.

The lesson from Kmart's saga is quintessential: Maintain focus, remain customer-centric, and ensure relevancy. This applies not only to the clientele but also to the workforce and collaborators. Sometimes, true disruptive innovation lies in revisiting and realigning with an organization's foundational values, listening to those closest to the consumer and keeping the customers at the heart of every decision.[76]

Xerox: A Missed Opportunity

The annals of tech history resonate with tales of breakthroughs and missed opportunities. Among the most compelling is Steve Jobs' visit to Xerox in 1979 as discussed earlier.

It began innocently enough. In Palo Alto, California, Xerox had quietly been fostering a hotbed of innovation at their research facility, Xerox PARC (Palo Alto Research Company). Conceived in 1970, Xerox's ambition for PARC was crystalline: usher in the technological future. Assembling a dream team named "The Architects of Information," this enclave of brilliance was led by Bob Taylor, who cultivated an environment where boundaries were redefined daily. John Warnock, a former Xerox PARC member, reminisced and said, "there was total intellectual freedom and no conventional wisdom, almost every idea was up for challenge."

To understand the sheer genius of this team, consider this: in the short span between 1970 and 1971, they pioneered laser printing. By 1972, they had revolutionized programming with object-oriented techniques. And 1973 saw the inception of the Xerox Alto PC. These advances, though revolutionary, were yet to be truly recognized by the larger tech community.

Enter Steve Jobs. By 1976, he and Steve Wozniak had launched Apple's first computer, setting the stage for Apple's meteoric rise. Fast-forward to 1979, and a deal between Apple and Xerox provided Jobs with a sneak peek into Xerox's latest innovations, notably the primitive "mouse" – a tool that promised to revolutionize user-computer interaction.

The sheer potential of this tool wasn't lost on Jobs. Witnesses recount his excitement, as he grasped the implications of this device as though he had discovered a treasure trove. While many at Xerox viewed these inventions as experimental pursuits, Jobs discerned their game-changing potential. In his eyes, Xerox sat on a goldmine, yet, curiously, lacked the vision to exploit it.

Reflecting on this later, Jobs famously remarked, "If Xerox had known what it had, and taken advantage of its real opportunities, it could have been as big as IBM plus Microsoft plus Xerox combined and the largest high-technology company in the world." This episode serves as a powerful reminder in the tech realm: true visionaries don't merely recognize innovation; they actualize its potential.[77,78]

Embrace the Power of Paranoia

Four iconic companies. Four cautionary tales underscoring the perils of complacency in an ever-evolving market. Their tales starkly illustrate the repercussions of ignoring disruption. It's not just about enduring turbulence; it's about survival. The thought behind disruption is that to metaphorically build an organization on rock, you must have the mindset that it is actually resting on sand.

Consistently think like this and disruption will be a living thing in your organization, like an organ in the body. Disruption must be present and living and breathing constantly. Because, if disruption dies, your organization may be close to its last breath. Can you hear the sound of the ventilator?

It's evident that complacency is an organization's silent nemesis. Xerox PARC's narrative highlights leadership's failure to articulate a clear mission or vision. The apprehension Xerox PARC felt during Jobs' visit wasn't misplaced. They were aware of the implications of a visionary like Jobs peeking behind their curtains. That visit bolstered Jobs' conviction that Apple was poised to reshape the digital frontier. The lesson here? Heed your frontline' insights. Guard your innovations. As Andy Groves aptly questions, "how do we know whether a change signals a strategic inflection point?" then answers... "The only way is through the process of clarification that comes from broad and intensive debate."[79]

Did any of these companies harness the strategic edge that a touch of paranoia might initiate collaboration? Evidently not. Could they have sidestepped their pitfalls? Without a doubt! Embracing a healthy dose of paranoia emboldens organizations, spurring them to undertake informed risks that yield long-term dividends. Predicting the future is riddled with unknowns. Yet, vested trust in your team, coupled with a discerning ear to the ground, can unveil pathways to success. Prioritize listening: to your team, the market, and most crucially, your customers. Noah Kerner and Gene Pressman's advice as stated in their book, *Chasing Cool*, serves a stern reminder: "You can get drunk on ego and wake up to a hangover of irrelevancy."[80]

Questioning the Standard

Disruption doesn't need to be the default approach but should be used as a basis for questioning the standard regularly. Without questioning the standard, organizations grow horizontally, with little potential for vertical growth.

Walt Disney never saw his films as a limitation. Rather, he envisioned Disneyland as an extension of his brand universe, bringing his film characters to life and adding another dimension of joy to the Disney experience. He also recognized the volatility of the film industry's profits. By introducing Disneyland, he could both capitalize on successes and mitigate the film sector's financial ebbs and flows. Many perceived Disney's plan as radical disruption. To him, it was simply "plus'ing" or enhancing the value offered to his audience.

Alvin Toffler's 1970s work, *Future Shock,* introduced the idea that societies might face paralysis and upheaval when confronted with overwhelming and rapid change. This kind of abrupt shift can lead to societal disarray, affecting core decision-making structures. Within any entity, be it a society or an organization, these ripple effects can deeply unsettle a firm's vision, mission, and values. While targeted disruption can clarify and reinvigorate these elements, an overwhelming change, or *future shock*, can introduce chaos. Therefore, when instigating change or disruption, it's crucial to maintain a balanced and strategic approach, ensuring that the core principles and objectives remain intact and shielded from detrimental external influences.

Leading with Vision

In *The Innovator's Dilemma,* Clayton Christensen pinpoints a compelling reason why historically successful organizations can stumble. He illustrates this through the chronicle of Sears, a retail powerhouse in the 1960s. Its decline was attributed largely to its management. Effective management disruption thrives when it is rooted in visionary leadership; absent this, frequent changes at the top can destabilize an entity. It's pivotal for management to grasp the foundational "why" from the outset.[81]

Marcelo Claure is a master at crafting organizations. He steered Brightstar to a commanding $6.3 billion sales figure in 2012 before its acquisition by SoftBank, which also owned Sprint. This move radically reshaped the global wireless service arena. Afterward, Claure transitioned to Sprint's board, eventually ascending to the CEO position in 2014.

Upon joining Sprint, Claure identified systemic issues – routines that had calcified and departments that functioned more like isolated silos. His response was methodical: study the company culture, streamline communication, and foster a culture of openness. He reshaped the organizational structure, initiated dialogue channels like the "Getting Better Every Day" and "Stupid Rules" emails, started daily sales and marketing meetings, implemented weekly staff meetings, moved executives to one floor where they could see each other in cubicle offices (remember Bob Noyce?), and focused on breaking down walls between departments. His reforms spurred positive change, rejuvenating Sprint's spirit and business trajectory after years of stagnation.[82,83]

Drawing inspiration from Malcolm Gladwell's iconic *Tipping Point,* successful leaders consistently showcase three critical attributes:

1. **Creativity:** Visionary leaders relentlessly seek improved or innovative solutions, always desiring an outcome superior to the status quo.
2. **Conscientiousness:** Rooted deeply in ethical considerations, conscientious leaders, and by extension their organizations, are driven by moral rectitude. This characteristic often finds its home within the value system of a company, guiding its path towards ethical and profitable growth.
3. **Constructive Dissent:** While the term "disagreeable" might sound negative, it's essential for a team to engage in constructive dissent. This promotes transparency and problem-solving, valuing mutual understanding over mere agreement.[84]

In essence, effective leadership isn't about adhering to past success models; it's about understanding when to challenge conventions, how to inspire collaboration, and the best way to steer an organization toward future successes.

"Everything that is great and inspiring, is created by individuals who can labor in freedom." Albert Einstein

Cadbury Care: Leading with Compassion

In 1824, John Cadbury, a young Quaker, began a modest venture in Birmingham, UK, dealing in tea, coffee, and cocoa beverages. Slowly transitioning from a small shop to a cocoa manufacturing unit, the company, named Cadbury, prospered until the 1850s. However, as the company's fortunes declined, his sons Richard and George joined in 1854 and took the helm in 1861, injecting their resources and energy into the then-struggling business.

George, valuing the quality that his father had always championed, was inspired after a trip to Holland, where he encountered a novel cocoa extraction technique at Van Houten. This method enhanced the chocolate's taste, making it "Absolutely pure... therefore Best," as their advertisements proudly claimed. By 1866, this innovation changed the tide and propelled Cadbury into a dominant position in the chocolate industry.

This journey from adversity to success is testament to the resilience and innovation of the Cadbury family. However, the Cadbury legacy is not just about chocolates. Despite being industry titans today, the Cadburys were also pioneering advocates for team member welfare.

The grim reality of the workforce in the 19th century included horrendous working conditions, abysmal wages, and virtually no consideration for workers' rights. Putting into perspective, the average work week was between 70 and 80 hours, the average pay was 1 shilling a day (.35 cents today). Children would work in factories alongside their parents if the family was too poor. Health conditions were unsanitary, and people were constantly sick, a team member worked until they died, there was no retirement. "Strapping" was a term used for hitting team members to wake them or make them work faster. Bottomline, the working environment was horrific.[85]

In this era, the Cadbury brothers chose a path of compassion. They envisioned an environment where their workers could thrive both professionally and personally. This led them to establish Bournville, a community designed for their team members. Spanning 330 acres, by 1900, it had 313 houses, a school, and a hospital. This village wasn't just about infrastructure; it symbolized trust, dedication, and a commitment to equality and well-being.

George Cadbury's philosophy was simple. He believed in a world where "each man could have his own house, a large garden to cultivate and healthy surroundings, ensuring a happier family life." Along with his second wife, Elizabeth, they spearheaded various initiatives, including introducing better working conditions, pensions, and philanthropic activities, solidifying Bournville's legacy. Their community also featured

The Beeches, a sanctuary for underprivileged children to enjoy their holidays.

The Cadbury family might have parted ways with their shares in the 1960s, but their legacy continues to reverberate in Bournville's community. The dedication, trust, and loyalty that the Cadburys fostered in their team members were not just corporate strategies; they were covenants of care and mutual respect.[86,87]

Indeed, when companies embed values of loyalty, trust, and dedication deeply within the fabric of the organization, they create a resilient workforce, ready to navigate challenges and emerge stronger and more growth-oriented.

At the heart of Open-Ended Logic organizations is an enduring commitment to team member development and growth. This isn't a mere strategy; it's the foundation for achieving long-term profitability growth. It's the team members who breathe life into products, cultivating lasting customer relationships. As Herb Kelleher, CEO of Southwest Airlines, aptly pointed out on April 15, 2003, "competitors might replicate tangible assets, but they can't replicate the *Southwest spirit... dedication, devotion, loyalty*—the sense that you are part of a greater mission."[88]

Magic happens when organizations pivot towards a team member-centric approach. It's this shift that can elevate a company from being merely good to truly exceptional. It's not just about offering benefits or incentives; it's about showing genuine care for team members' lives, both within and outside the office confines. While not every organization can build physical communities like Cadbury's Bournville, investing in fostering a sense of belonging and community in the workplace can yield immeasurable returns. Don't you want that magic? I do. We all do. But those who obtain it are the ones who crave it enough to intentionally prioritize it.

The Power of Thoughtful Pause

The power to think freely is not just a luxury; it's an essential catalyst that can steer a team, organization, or business in the right direction. But how do we set the wheels of thought into motion? It involves creating space to deliberate on the vision, mission, and various components integral to a company's success.

One might wonder, with everyone so immersed in thought, who's handling the day-to-day tasks? The objective is not about sidelining action but about allocating specific timeframes for deliberate reflection. This doesn't solely apply to the upper echelons of management. True innovation often emerges from those at the grassroots level, the frontline team members who often possess transformative insights about their specific realms.

Consider Jeff Weiner, the acclaimed CEO of LinkedIn. His daily routine carves out an impressive two hours dedicated purely to thinking. This regimen emerged from a need to break free from his continual string of meetings. Initially, these slots served as mere breathers, but over time, they transformed into pivotal periods essential for his leadership effectiveness.

> *As the organization gets larger, so too will the frequency of those [challenging] issues, yet there remains only one of you. Unless you can coach others to address challenges directly, you will quickly find yourself in a position where that's all you're doing (adding even more meetings to your day). That's no way to run a team or a company.*

Jeff Weiner[89]

Weiner believes that as a company grows, its leadership must also evolve dynamically. Staying ahead of the curve is paramount, ensuring proactive decision-making rather than reactive responses. As he suggests, leaders must cultivate a proactive mindset rather than being continually reactive.

So, what should one ponder during these periods of reflection? Envision the organization's trajectory in the near future and the long run. Strategically identify initiatives that promise significant impact and potential profitability. Prioritize both the company and its customers. Set your sights on that paramount objective.

Adam Grant, in his book *Originals*, eloquently suggests that brilliance can't always be rushed. As Leonardo da Vinci noted, sometimes the most ingenious ideas form during moments of pause, where perfection is visualized and crafted in the mind. It's a testament to the undeniable power of giving thought its deserved time and space.[90]

The Art of Thoughtful Decision-Making

Sometimes, an overload of information can lead to paralysis by analysis. Surprisingly, some of the most effective decisions arise when we possess just 35 percent of the available data.

Take Walt Disney as an example. In February 1928, after an unexpected and unsettling business turn, Disney found himself on a long train journey from New York to Los Angeles. He had attempted to renew a contract for Oswald the Lucky Rabbit, his creation. Instead, he was outmaneuvered by Charles Mintz (who had married Margaret Winkler, the owner of the Oswald character rights). Mintz not only took control of Oswald but was also actively luring away Disney's artists. (Sidenote: the nefarious character in the movie *Up* was inspired by Charles Mintz.)[91]

Despite the setbacks, Disney wasn't one to dwell on the past. Upon reaching California, rather than being bogged down by over-analysis, he tapped into the essence of what had made Oswald popular. He recognized that while other animations of the era were often rigid and bleak, his creations were anchored in storytelling. This realization, combined with the creative input of a small, dedicated team including his wife, Lillian, led to the birth of an iconic character we know and love today: Mickey Mouse. Disney's approach showcases the power of intuitive decision-making. Instead of succumbing to overthought, he drew insights from his past successes and charted a course for the future.

The Power of Decentralized Decision-Making

Embracing Open-Ended Logic means cultivating an environment of autonomy within an organization. When this approach is truly integrated, decisions bubble up from the grassroots level rather than being imposed from the top down. Companies that determine budgets, marketing strategies, or customer-oriented measures strictly from a top-down perspective often miss the mark - a lot! Assuming that those furthest from the customer should dictate customer-related decisions is fundamentally flawed.

Those in direct contact to the consumer are the crown jewels and organizations realizing this that place value on them are often more aligned with their needs, leading to more accurate and effective initiatives, programs, and solutions.

Case in point - Avis, recognized for its clever "We're #2, so we try harder" ad campaign. Yet, the transformative leadership of CEO Robert Townsend (1962-1965) is what set Avis apart during its time. Like Bob Noyce, Townsend defied conventional leadership norms. Many regard him as the progenitor of Egalitarian Leadership. Townsend was an advocate for the "Theory Y" management style: trust your team members and let them work with minimal oversight. His book, *Up the Organization*, outlines the Commandments of Business, emphasizing decision-making that involves input from all organizational levels.

The Townsend principles upheld were:

- No reserved parking spaces
- No org charts
- No job descriptions
- No short-term pandering to Wall Street
- No company planes
- No golf club memberships
- Stock options for everybody
- Honesty is the best policy
- Reinvestment for the long haul
- Rewards for performance
- Commitment to product (service) quality
- True delegation
- Encouragement of healthy dissent
- Virtue of putting customers first[92]

Townsend argued that top-down decisions aren't inherently wrong, but without insights from those on the ground, a company would inevitably become disconnected and lose team member engagement.

One classic example of a misstep was Blockbuster's attempt to rival Netflix. Despite making initial moves that could have made them competitive, including a $200 million investment in Blockbuster Online and eliminating a significant revenue stream from late fees, leadership changes halted these initiatives, contributing to their bankruptcy in 2010.[93]

Townsend believed in discerning between significant and minor decisions, suggesting swift decisions for lesser matters. He was a visionary in his time, dismantling the corporate hierarchies and trusting team members to deliver. Like other leaders of his ilk, such as Noyce and Disney, he believed in fostering a space for ideas to flourish. Without a culture that encourages open dialogue, trust, and innovation, organizations will likely stagnate and fail to realize their full potential.

Be Curious

Incumbents have been slow to adapt, and they continue to try to make people want things while upstart brands have recognized the power of making things people want.

Bernadette Jiwa

Meaningful: The story of Ideas That Fly

The Birth of Imagineering — Cultivating a Curiosity Mindset

Walt Disney Productions, riding the wave of its animated movie successes, started evolving into the vast entertainment conglomerate Walt had always envisioned. At the heart of this evolution lay the concept of *"Imagineering"*, a mixture of "imagination" and "engineering". Walt created this term when he realized he needed a specialized team — a blend of artists and engineers — to design and construct what would be known as Disneyland. In December 1952, he assembled a select group of artists from his studio division, assigning them a mission to turn his amusement park dream into reality.

This fledgling team of Imagineers transformed into a separate entity known as WED Enterprises, an acronym honoring its founder, Walt Elias Disney. Situated in a rented space at Disney's Burbank Studios, this venture, fully owned by Walt, was a sandbox for creativity without boundaries.

In the book *Lead like Walt*, Pat Williams recounts an interaction with Harriet Burns, a revered Disney figure and early Imagineer. She reminisced about Walt laying out the expansive vision of Disneyland and then empowering the Imagineers to fill in the details. He encouraged them with the sentiment that "The dream is wide open!"

Empowering the Imagineering team with autonomy and encouraging audacious curiosity and boundless creativity made WED Enterprises a hive of innovation and excitement. Even though Walt was yet to finalize Disneyland's location or gather resources for its construction, he possessed a firm belief that each idea would lead to the next, progressively moving him closer to his vision. He ensured that his team members shared this vision, driving them to actualize it each day.

Disney's knack for translating dreams into reality, one step at a time, underscores his genius. Every layered concept started with an idea, which he relentlessly pursued. Fueled by curiosity, he led his team on an uncharted journey. The Imagineers, despite lacking any prior experience in amusement park construction, were given free rein to brainstorm and visualize Disneyland, making use of storyboards to capture their innovative ideas. Their unbridled creativity enabled them to envision an unparalleled fantasy realm.

With Disneyland's design in place, the team shifted their focus to the necessary technology. In their innovation lab, they pioneered animatronics for iconic attractions like "It's A Small World" and "Pirates of the Caribbean". As rival theme parks sprouted in the 1960s, Disney maintained its commitment to quality, setting the gold standard for a magical experience where imagination knew no bounds.[94]

Nurturing Curiosity: The Foundation for Progress

Ideas often arise in the most unexpected moments. Google CMO, Lorraine Twohill, suggests that moments of brilliance can strike during a gym session, under the shower, or even during casual chats and gatherings. Recalling the informal meetings at Fairchild and later Intel, one is reminded of how fostering an environment ripe for curiosity provides an unmatched return on investment. It's not about orchestrated group thinking, but rather about allowing organic discussions that initiate productive and imaginative insights, creating a sense of fulfillment.

In our younger years, we question everything, from the colors of nature to the physics behind daily occurrences. But as we age, our inherent curiosity tends to rein in, overshadowed by the fear of being inquisitive. Reflecting on LinkedIn's approach, CEO As discussed earlier, Jeff Weiner dedicates up to two hours daily for contemplation, a ritual that exemplifies how nurturing curiosity can lead to groundbreaking ideas. True curiosity is often ignited by persistent leaders who frequently ask "Why?", always aiming to unearth solutions to complex problems.

If an organization isn't fostering curiosity, it's already stagnating - and stagnation isn't being still, it's the process of working backwards to corrosiveness, a precursor to absolute irrelevance.

Back in 1962, amidst significant historical events, Phil Knight began selling shoes from his car's trunk, marking the inception of what would later become Nike. Right from its embryonic stage, Nike championed the spirit of curiosity. As a testament to this, even when Nike had soared to a $33 billion company, former CEO Mark Parker remained actively engaged in every facet of the business. According to *Chasing Cool* by Noah Kerner and Gene Pressman, Nike always maintains a finger on the pulse, understanding its consumers at an intimate level.

Nike's journey is a testament to how curiosity can fuel success. From Phil Knight's initial focus on running shoes to partnering with revered coach Bill Bowerman, Nike always prioritized innovation. Early on, the team was obsessed with enhancing their "Tigers" shoe designs, emphasizing quality and durability. Their Japanese manufacturer, Onitsuka, misread Nike's commitment to excellence as a threat, leading them to compete directly. The outcome? Onitsuka remained relatively obscure, while Nike soared to global acclaim.[95]

Nike's ascent can be attributed to a mix of relentless drive, veracious tenacity, and a persistent dedication to curiosity. Without this potent combination, it would not have attained its current stature.

True curiosity requires immersing oneself in the world, absorbing everything it has to offer, and continuously questioning to nurture growth. Organizations must recalibrate their approach and instill an ever-curious conduit, open-minded, and learning-focused mindset in their team members.

The Curious Case of Creativity

The following comes from the *Think with Google* page titled "The Curious Case of Creativity," written by Google's then-VP of Marketing (current Chief Marketing Officer) Lorraine Twohill in April 2012. It confirms the reasons for Google's success and continued pursuit of curiosity and creativity.

> *Good ideas sell products. Great ideas change lives. From opening up our brand to opening up museums, we see creativity as a way to solve problems - large and small. Lorraine Twohill, Google VP of Global Marketing, explains how:*
>
> *Engineers see the world differently. While most of us accept what we see or adapt to our environments, an engineer wonders 'Why?' Why are things the way they are? Why can't we change them? This passion for solving problems drives a lot of our creative thinking at Google. We aspire to be a company*

that tackles issues that affect billions of people, whether they're small, everyday concerns or huge, global-scale problems.

Curiosity and creativity are never far apart. You need to be curious to identify problems worth solving, and then come up with new solutions. We try to foster this in the Google culture. Our teams are full of curious, energetic, passionate people from diverse backgrounds, and they have unconventional approaches to work, play, and life. Our atmosphere may be casual, but as new ideas emerge – at lunch, on campus, in the gym – they are traded, tested, and put into practice with dizzying speed. Often these ideas become launch pads for new projects destined for worldwide use.

We don't just solve problems with our software, but also with our marketing. Ultimately, we want to help people understand how technology can enhance their lives, letting them spend time doing more important things than reading a manual. To do that, we remind ourselves to constantly ask 'why' and keep a few rules of thumb in mind: Focus on one real person, be open, say yes, and have a purpose.

In a world where everything we do is counted in the billions (clicks, visits, users), it's easy to think solely in terms of numbers and digits. That's why we try to focus on one real person. That real person could be your mom, your brother, or your friend. Boiling technology down to a simple message focusing on real benefits that matter to people, can make a product personal. It shows people how technology connects to and enhances their daily lives. It's not always easy; people are more complex than machines, after all. We certainly don't get it right every time, but our best creative work carries a simple yet meaningful message. Our 'Dear Sophie' ad for Chrome shows how one person – a new dad – can use the web to share memories with his daughter as she grows up.

We embrace creativity all around us. Ideas can come from anyone, not just a 'Creative' department. We open-source ideas internally, and we also collaborate with many content creators, artists, developers, brands, agencies, and people who come to us with wonderful ideas. They stretch and inspire us. Collaboration is essential to problem-solving in our increasingly complex world. That is why we believe so strongly in the power of open technologies and platforms. They enable anyone, anywhere, to apply their unique skills, perspectives, and passions to the creation of new products and features on top of our platforms.

Whether helping a small business owner, a new dad, or a kid who wants to learn more, it's a healthy disregard for the impossible that compels us to find creative solutions to all sorts of problems.

One of our initiatives, 'Chrome Experiments,' encourages interesting uses of HTML5 on our Chrome browser. Perhaps the most well-known experiment to come out of this is The Wilderness Downtown, an interactive multimedia video set to music from Arcade Fire. It was a collaboration between the band, our Data Arts team and writer/director Chris Milk. The project wasn't about the technology. It was about how we could use technology to redefine the music video experience. Because let's face it, not a lot has changed since MTV debuted 'Video Killed the Radio Star' almost 30 years ago.

There are plenty more examples, for which we can take very little credit. Through Google+, artists like will.i.am from the Black-Eyed Peas, and singer-songwriter Daria Musk, are re-imagining what a live concert can be. Sal Khan is using the YouTube platform to revolutionize a system of education that has barely changed in two centuries. In 2006, the former hedge fund analyst began remotely tutoring family members, posting video lessons for them to watch in their own time, at their own pace. Since then, his 'Khan Academy' has grown into an online collection of over 3,000 educational videos with a total of 1.3 billion views and 3.6 million subscribers. They are fun, clever, and incredibly creative. For Khan, they all started as a solution to a problem: How can I schedule tutoring sessions around work, soccer practice, and different time zones?

Creativity can also be a decision you make. And the truth is, it's too easy to say 'no' all the time. It's too easy to be cautious. Pushing the boundaries of creativity means saying 'yes,' taking risks, trying new things, learning, and being surprised. So, we don't just open-source ideas at Google, we open-source our brand.

Every day, illustrators and engineers create beautiful interpretations of our logo, and we display these 'Doodles' on our homepage. For a number of years, one of my favorite marketing programs has been Doodle 4 Google. It is a competition that asks students to design a Doodle around a theme such as 'Our Community' or 'My Future.' No one is more creative than kids, and this contest drives that home for me every year. By inviting users of all ages to share their imagination, we ultimately share ownership of our brand.

It wasn't a coincidence that we released the beta version of Gmail, offering one GB of free storage, on April Fool's Day, 2004. That much storage is normal now, but at the time no one else came close, so people thought we were joking. When they realized we weren't, it was a delightful surprise and also a huge story. We didn't do it with a flashy ad, we did it with a decision. Similarly, we chose to license the little green Android robot under Creative Commons, meaning anyone can do whatever they want with it. This has helped the immense success of Android and has also fostered an incredible momentum of creative energy all over the world.[96]

Creativity is most powerful when it has a purpose. Through projects at Google, we have opened up the world's best museums (Art Project), helped kids develop a love of science (Google Science Fair and YouTube Space Lab), showed how much we all have in common (Life in a Day), and brought small businesses onto the web (Getting America's Businesses Online). We have a strong sense of why we exist and why we do what we do. We believe that our legacy – as a company and as individuals – should be to make a difference in the world around us.

Fostering Curiosity: The Catalyst for Forward Momentum

Lorraine Twohill's memo underscores an important recruitment principle: regardless of the department, a candidate's curiosity standard should be a benchmark. It's not merely about technical prowess or experience; it's about having the passion to explore, learn, and innovate, vital for any organization aiming to maintain market relevance.

Historically, Disney was a model of stimulating curiosity. In a time when instant digital knowledge wasn't at one's fingertips, Walt Disney sought to create an environment that would continually spark creativity. Around 1930, he launched an initiative to amass thousands of books, filled with artistic works from around the world, to create a reservoir of inspiration – a creative library. Moreover, he instituted evening classes, partnering with esteemed professors to enhance the skills of his in-house artists.

Recognizing the synergy of collaborative creativity, Walt engaged renowned artists not just for specific projects but to foster a pervasive culture of curiosity. Knowing that these art legends were accessible for brainstorming and feedback propelled Disney artists to explore new creative terrains. This proactive environment set the stage for masterpieces like Snow White and the Seven Dwarfs.

> *"For the poet is a light winged and holy thing, and there is no invention in him until he has been inspired and is out of his senses and the mind is no longer with him. When he has not attained this state, he is powerless and unable to utter his oracles."*
>
> Plato[97,98]

Heed Herbert Gerjuoy's prophetic words: *"Tomorrow's illiterate will not be the man who cannot read; he will be the man who has not learned how to learn"* is correct, curiosity correlates directly to our intellect, knowledge, and growth. Are we courageous enough to ask the next question, willing to learn more -- to be curious? With this dose of courage, we'll open more doors of possibility within our organizations, team members, and customers. Curiosity inspires us and, in us, creates the power to utter our oracles.[99]

In sales, for instance, curiosity is pivotal. Sales personnel who dive deeper with questions can truly understand client needs, offering tailored solutions that resonate. This same inquisitive mindset, when applied universally across an organization, can unlock unparalleled potential.

Perhaps the surge of business consultation and outsourcing can be attributed to a growing curiosity deficit within companies. Organizations may stagnate due to:

- Insufficient introspection time
- Lack of training or upskilling opportunities
- Disengagement from the company's vision and values
- An environment lacking open, honest dialogue
- A reluctance to take calculated risks
- A misunderstanding of the profound importance of curiosity

Being fundamentally aligned with an organization's core, the curiosity to understand, improve, and seize opportunities becomes a conscious action instead of a forced reaction. It becomes a natural extension of thoughts and conversations both inside and outside the four walls of your organization – even your desk.

"The greatest threat to curiosity is the extinction of dialogue." Seth Goldenberg[100]

Without curiosity, organizations become stagnant and eventually fail. When Michael Eisner and Frank Wells took over Disney in 1984, the company was in disarray and falling apart. Curiosity had all but disappeared. When Eisner arrived with enthusiasm and questions of how, who and why, it turned the company upside down for the better — a complete disruption. Since Walt's passing almost 20 years prior, Disney had been operating in the past with mediocre to dismal results. Eisner wanted to turn hotels into buildings that replicated Mickey himself. Ideas of all kinds were suddenly evolving, and "poof"—curiosity was once again floating through the halls of Disney like pixie dust.

Ultimately, nurturing curiosity is transformative. When cultivated and channeled correctly, it not only revitalizes an organization's mission but also galvanizes its team, pushing boundaries and setting the stage for unprecedented success.

Opening New Doors Creates Curiosity

We were lucky enough to grow up in an environment where there was always much encouragement to children to pursue intellectual interests; to investigate whatever aroused curiosity.

Wilbur & Orville Wright

Walt said, "There's really no secret about our approach. We keep moving – opening up new doors and doing new things – because we're curious. And curiosity keeps leading us down new paths. We're always exploring and experimenting."[101]

The Curiosity of Burbn

Ever heard of Burbn? For those who tried the app in 2010, they discovered a platform aimed at documenting users' locations and sharing details, including photos and rewards points, particularly at places offering, aptly, bourbon. However, post-launch, the app's flaws became apparent. It was cluttered and far from user-friendly.

Kevin Systrom, Burbn's founder, discerningly recognized these pitfalls. He partnered with Mike Krieger and together they undertook a meticulous analysis of user activity within the app. Among Burbn's myriad features, they identified one that stood out: "photo sharing." It emerged as a focal point, with users keen on sharing snaps of not just their drink orders, but a broader spectrum of their experiences. Observing this trend, Systrom and Krieger made a strategic choice to zero in on this feature.

Drawing inspiration and learning from apps like Hipstamatic and even giants like Facebook, the duo discerned key elements that defined success in the photo-sharing domain. Their keen observation revealed that, despite its might, Facebook lagged in this specific feature. Their inquisitiveness spotlighted a niche where they could refine and perfect the photo-sharing experience.

Rebranding Burbn to the now-iconic "Instagram," the app made its debut on October 6, 2010. Its instant appeal was evident. Within a single day, it amassed 25,000 users, ballooning to a million within three months. The meteoric rise of Instagram did not escape notice; celebrities hopped onto the bandwagon, further boosting its profile. Initially pigeonholed as a mere photo-sharing app, Instagram soon emerged as a potent social platform. Systrom rightly boasted in March 2012, "It's Facebook-level engagement that we're seeing." In a short span of two years, Instagram's user base surged to nearly 50 million, catching the eye of Facebook's Mark Zuckerberg, who acquired it for a modest $1 billion compared to its estimated valuation of well over $40 billion today.[102]

The metamorphosis of Burbn into the global phenomenon Instagram was no accident. It was the outcome of Systrom and Krieger's relentless curiosity. Had they chosen to be complacent, Burbn might have faded into oblivion. This tale underscores the power of curiosity: it can illuminate the microscopic detail that, when honed, can revolutionize a brand, aligning it seamlessly with its overarching vision.

Be curious! Get after it! If you don't, just remember there's a fearless 17-year-old out there brimming with audacity, lethal to the core, Red Bull in hand, full of curiosity, ready to disrupt the world.

Predictable Outcomes

What do we, as discerning consumers, truly seek when engaging in commerce? Simple—a good, predictable outcome.

Success is peace of mind, which is a direct result of self-satisfaction in knowing you made the effort to become the best you are capable of becoming.

John Wooden

Predictable – able to be foretold or declared in advance. (dictionary.com)

Predictable – expected, certain, calculable, foreseeable. (thesaurus.com)

Predictability can be both a good thing or a bad thing. We have good experiences and bad experiences. If the experience is good, we go back. If the experience is bad, we avoid it or we suck it up and deal with it and wait for a better option. If we are the customer, in most cases, we hold the upper hand. As consumers, we often feel like we're in the driver's seat. There are instances where entities, like local agencies or government services, might seem immune to our preferences. Still, even these units are undergoing transformative changes in response to customer expectations - because we now have options (e.g., Post Office).

However, even when we don't control an entity's decision, we hold the ultimate decision: to either become a customer or not. That decision is lightly wound around the predictability of our experience of the brand. One experience does not always constitute a predictable outcome for the next, which leads us to ask... how many experiences does it take for a consumer to believe they will receive a predictable outcome?

Before diving directly into the realm of predictability, it's crucial to define the desired outcome we want. We need to know what it looks, feels, and maybe even, smells like.

Desire – to wish or long for. (dictionary.com)

Desire – aspiration, appetite, craving, devotion, motive, passion, wish, yearning. (thesaurus.com)

We know what we desire; now how do we make this predictable?

Desire encapsulates wishes, cravings, yearnings, and motivations. We're not just passive recipients of our experiences; we crave specific sensations and outcomes. Be it the familiar taste of our morning coffee or the thrill of entering Disneyland, our desires shape our expectations.

Now, let's consider desire and predictability from the perspective of the routine service experiences in our everyday lives, like when we walk into the bank or corner convenience store. As a guest, we seek acknowledgment—a nod, a greeting, a smile. These small gestures reinforce the feeling of being valued. The simple ways brands can foster trust and loyalty. We think, "I'm here, let me know you see me." We appreciate a delivery person whose smile conveys they recognize we chose their company when there are so many other options to choose from. But getting to this predictable state requires knowing what it is we want—our desired state. Once we understand the desired outcome, the process begins to make that desired outcome then predictable.

Predictability stems from our ingrained habits. Our day-to-day consists of repeating a thousand habits over and over again and tend to gravitate towards familiar experiences, seeking consistency and dependability. It breaks down to mindsets. Our minds are locked and loaded to stick with habits, which means to break a habit, we require logic to educate us as to why that habit needs to be replaced, updated, or eliminated. This is why strong brands continually refine their customer interactions, striving to offer experiences that are both positive and consistent.

Forming good habits is great, but they're hard to maintain without understanding why those habits are formed in the first place. Habitually eating well is the genesis of feeling good and having a healthy body. If your mind is set on the predictable outcome, the probability of success is much greater.

A brand reaches the pinnacle of success when a customer forms the habit of incorporating that brand into their life. This means that brands and their companies can become a habit if the consumer predictably relies on their services and products. Bad predictable outcomes are absorbed by good predictable outcomes and vice versa. Every experience creates a predictable outcome in the mind of the customer.

What this means for organizations, groups, and teams is that we must deliver consistent predictable outcomes every time. This is the only way to sustain a positive predictable outcome in the mind of the consumer. The question is, what do you want the predictable outcome to be? And what are the steps to forming a true predictable outcome for your customers or guests, as Disney calls their customers? The predictable outcome is not a one-time event but a predictable experience that leads to a consumer's long-term commitment.

When we order something from Amazon, we click "buy," and we usually receive the order the next day if we're a Prime subscriber. This is predictability. Go to Starbucks and order a Grande Caramel Macchiato upside-down on ice with two shots of vanilla and whipped cream. Predictability means it should taste the same every time. Go to Aldi's and find fruit on sale. Predictability. Have Paradigm Shift deliver leadership and development training that truly creates positive change. Predictable. Call Zappos and get a live person in customer service, fast, who *wants* to help. That's predictability!

What would be predictable in a Craigslist experience? Nothing. Craigslist outcomes are extremely unpredictable.

- Craigslist **buyer**: must ensure safety first by meeting at a well-lit, high traffic area; see the goods, accept the goods, and pay the seller for the goods.
- Craigslist **seller**: must ensure safety first by meeting at a well-lit, high traffic area; show your goods and get paid for your goods. Determine ahead of time how to get paid (Venmo or cash, etc.).

There are simply more steps involved with an unpredictable outcome, thus creating a more expensive transaction in terms of time and energy. In Stephen M. R. Covey's book, The Speed of Trust, it is determined, both psychologically and monetarily, that the "cost" of trust is extremely high when trust is low, and the "cost" of trust is low when trust is high.[103]

When a business cares more about a customer's predictable outcome, leadership discovers the ingredients of a great predictable outcome and infuses these strategies into their people. When customers don't have to think twice about the outcome, the brand is winning another day.

Zappos entered the world in 1999 with the idea that when a customer orders a pair of shoes online, they should receive them quickly. What Zappos added was not only fast shipping but a customer service experience that made a wonderfully predictable buying experience with phenomenal, off-the-chart customer support. Zappos states on their About Us page that "at Zappos.com, our purpose is simple: to live and deliver WOW." Here's how Zappos sees the future of retail.

- One day, 30 percent of all retail transactions in the U.S. will be online
- People will buy from the company with the best service and the best selection
- Zappos.com will be that online store

Zappos created the predictable experience of exceptional customer service. When a customer orders a particular pair of shoes, they're not only receiving them quickly, but they'll have a satisfaction guarantee to count on. If the customer does not want to keep the shoes, they can be shipped back, no questions asked, for a full refund. This is a predictable service that helps create a long-term profitable customer. Zappos has created a predictable buying experience that is repeatable and scalable without relying on sales and the best price syndrome to which so many organizations fall victim.[104]

Predictability is the result of one mindset centered around the vision. Zappos' vision is simple and understandable for everyone who works there: the development team posting the product, the customer service team receiving the calls, the fulfillment team, and the shipping company (another extension of any organization). Each leg of the process works in unison and is in alignment with the vision - deliver happiness.

When looking at price competitiveness and predictable outcomes, what generates more revenue and creates a long-term profitable business? Predictable outcomes give organizations the ability to not concentrate so much on "best price" but rather on "best service," thus creating long-term sustainable customers. By owning predictable outcomes, the business can deliver A+ service. In order of importance to customers, price is third or, in some cases, fourth on the list. In most, if not all, industries, service is the number-one attribute that consistently wins customers over. The word "service" is a broad and audacious term if you look at it from the lens of the consumer. It encompasses website user experience, the call with customer service or sales, IT support, and a vast number of intricate areas where customers communicate with the organization. It determines if a customer returns or not.

We are a society that gravitates to what we know. Our minds are wired to be systematic in process and generally take the road most traveled. We want what we know, and if an organization convinces us that a service or product is consistently great, we're hooked.

We all have habits of predictability, such as a bedtime routine: brushing our teeth, checking in with the kids, saying a prayer, reading before laying our heads on the pillow, etc. These are human behaviors of a predictable nature, and, as already mentioned, there are hundreds, if not thousands, of habits we do without thought every day. Take smartphones—phone companies have convinced us there is a predictable outcome when we turn our phones on, so much so that the smartphone has not just become part of our day but is embedded in our lives. We use it for personal and business reasons minute-by-minute. It has proven to be predictable in our lives in the sense that we can count on it for staying in tune with our day-to-day tasks. We can, as well, stay in tune with everyone else. Consumers align with brands that offer positive, predictable outcomes to avoid the uncertainty of negative results. This is why strong brands routinely strive to avoid complacency.

Joplin Emergency Management in Joplin, Missouri, set up a process around people, management on the ground, and property. With unpredictable surroundings, they initiated a process that set things in motion for a predictably organized outcome through preparation and dealt systemically with little flaws through an unpredictable disastrous event.

Predictive intelligence is also a game changer in the information we analyze through data systems and algorithms. Everyone wants to know the future, and whoever has pinpointed it correctly has created wealth. At the time of this writing, there were over 103,000,000 results for "Predictive Intelligence" on Google.

Organizations have perhaps two shots to prove that they are a predictable resource. First, they must prove they are good at one or more things embedded in their values and missions, and second, they must duplicate the first experience of great service. For some consumers, it may take multiple experiences for a company to prove itself predictable. There are too many things to think about during the day. Predictability removes the noise in the brain: A consumer doesn't have to remember why "I don't like going to X establishment" or why "I like going to Y establishment"—the brain's "muscle memory" leads them to the place they enjoy the most and feel the best. Consumers love predictable outcomes because they require less brainpower.

Why does Chick-fil-A have predictable outcomes? They've built processes that make predictable outcomes happen. In-fact, Chick-fil-A predicts very well. When they noted long lines in the drive thru, they predicted that if lines moved faster, more customers would come - they simply removed the friction points. Then they equipped drive-thru teammates with iPads to take orders and charge customers' credit cards before they reached the window. This adjustment reduced steps from the drive thru process and made it more efficient. After a smile and the "thank you for your business" and "you can pull forward now" dialogue, the customer proceeds quickly to the drive-thru window. And with the pleasantries of "thank you" and "my pleasure," plus double-checking the order, Chick-fil-A's cycle of predictability is complete for another guest. Chick-fil-A operates with consistent curiosity and research, learning about their customers' behaviors to deliver more predictable outcomes. This is the not-so-secret secret to their success.

In essence, predictability is a foundational pillar for businesses. It becomes a pillar of the structure, establishing a blueprint for purpose-driven day-to-day work. This allows culture to thread individuals closer to the mission and vision.

What are the necessary ingredients?

Time + energy + attention to detail = a repeatable, scalable, predictable outcome

The Challenge of Crafting Predictable Outcomes

So, why aren't more organizations jockeying for more predictable outcomes? Risk aversion. Predictable outcomes, conversions, strategies, and plans cannot remove risks. This is the challenge.

The answer is simple: fear of risk. While strategies, conversations, and plans aim for predictable results, they can't entirely avert uncertainties. Crafting predictable outcomes demands significant time, preparation, rigorous training, and a relentless focus on organizational awareness. However, navigating through these challenges can be less daunting by concentrating on specific aspects of business one at a time. Gabriel Weinberg and Justin Mares, in their book *Traction*, highlight that while risks are inevitable, they can be mitigated by honing in on one business channel at a time. Success, they argue, is a product of the concentrated effort and commitment directed towards perfecting one channel until its outcomes become predictable. Once that's achieved, organizations can transition to the next channel, ensuring continuous improvement and stability.[105]

Pursuing the Predictable Outcome

Is everything predictable? Absolutely not. Expecting a predictable outcome without first defining the outcome is ludicrous, yet most operations do exactly this and become counterproductive. They aim for consistent results without clarifying what should be consistent. When steps are documented and methodologies outlined, outcomes become more foreseeable, thus facilitating process leadership. When these processes are adhered to, the likelihood of achieving the desired outcome increases.

Should processes be so structured that they lack flexibility and human touch? Not if they empower individuals, especially those interfacing closest with consumers, to deliver exceptional service – take Zappos as an example.

How can we set expectations of excellence from team members if we don't specify what *"excellence"* implies? We often find organizations demanding top-notch performance without giving a clear picture of what that means -- what it actually looks and feels like. Identifying excellence requires a process for achieving repeatable predictability within our products, services, and most crucially, our people.

Starbucks offers a case in point. They train their baristas not just in crafting the perfect cup of coffee, but also in handling challenging situations and difficult guests. In today's fast-paced society, consumers want both uniqueness in their coffee choices and speedy service. When they anticipate a certain service level, any deviation can lead to dissatisfaction. But with the right training, like that provided to Starbucks baristas, even when things go awry, the experience can be steered back towards a predictable positive outcome.

The Aggregation of Marginal Gains

Smiling is marginal.

Sir David Brailsford
British Cycling Performance Director & Coach[106]

For over one-hundred years, the British Cycling team was considered one of the worst cycling teams in history. The Tour de France began in 1903, but the British team didn't win the esteemed, legendary race nor had they been a major force in the cycling arena since the 1908 Olympic Games, when several British cyclists at one time, won medals, until Sir David Brailsford became the Director of Performance and coach in 2003.[107]

For context, what does *"the aggregation of marginal gains"* really mean?

Aggregation – a collection of various distinct elements

Marginal gains – the theory that small yet significant improvements can lead to monumental results.[108]

The term *"marginal gains"* will resonate as a testament and articulate a given name for what you already believe you're doing or will be an inspiring philosophy that will increase sustainable performance for your personal development, your team, and your organization from here on.[109]

Brailsford created the "aggregation of marginal gains" concept by approaching it as a mathematical equation. "Margin" is indeed a financial term. Like compound interest, a 1 percent increase year over year will lead to a larger gain over time. Therefore, Brailsford theorized, if a business increases their margins by adding positive gains or reducing areas of diminishing returns, he could apply the same principle to his cycling team. He was convinced that the aggregation of those hundreds, if not thousands, of little things would increase performance and that it became "prescriptive" in that if specific actions (X) were taken, desired outcomes (Y) would be achieved—this, then that. In essence, the aggregation of marginal gains is dissecting the process down into individual parts, refining each component by 1 percent, integrating these improvements and repackaging into the aggregate.

In practice, the team adopted numerous subtle changes: optimizing seat comfort, having surgeons train hand-washing techniques to minimize illnesses, selecting the best bedding for optimal sleep, and even painting their transport vans white to spot and address minuscule dirt particles on their bikes that would normally go unnoticed. These meticulous details, regularly reinforced, became foundational to their strategy. Brailsford was confident that this approach would yield predictable, positive outcomes.

Brailsford's theory was that if they began implementing the aggregation of marginal gains, it would result in predictable outcomes.

His theory bore fruit. By 2008, the British team clinched 60 percent of the cycling golds at the Beijing Olympics. Their staggering success continued: in 2012, they established nine Olympic and seven world records. That same year, Bradley Wiggins secured the British team's inaugural Tour de France victory. Subsequent victories in 2013, 2015, 2016, and 2017 under Chris Froome further solidified their dominance. From 2007 to 2017, the British Cycling team accumulated 178 World Championships, sixty-six Olympic or Paralympic golds, and triumphed in five Tour de France races.

While celebrating these achievements, it's pivotal to acknowledge the transitional period between 2003, when Brailsford took charge, and 2007, when the team's transformation began to manifest. This period underscores the importance of patience, persistence, and the belief in a vision, even when results aren't immediately apparent.

The Waterwheel Principle

Spanning roughly five years from when Brailsford began applying his marginal gains theory to when the cycling team began to see tangible success might seem short in a broad perspective. Still, on a closer examination, it may appear that progress was slow in coming. Brailsford's assertion that "it's pretty evident this works," highlights the British Cycling team's sustained victories over the past two decades. However, in the initial stages, there might have been moments of doubt. Perhaps the initial indicators of success were subtle, seen only in stopwatch measurements or in the enhanced morale and optimism stemming from a renewed approach.

The principle can be likened to the workings of a waterwheel. When the concept of marginal gains is initiated, broken down into manageable 1 percent tasks, its immediate impact might be faint. But collectively, these small improvements have a considerable cumulative effect.

Historically, the waterwheel, dating back to as early as 400 BC, stands as one of humanity's first devices generating mechanical energy autonomously, superseding manual labor and beasts of burden. Primarily used for tasks like grain grinding, its mechanism is simple yet profound. For the waterwheel to function, it relies on a steady flow of water. Initially, this flow might not seem to influence the wheel's movement. However, as water continues to pour, the wheel starts its rotation, gradually increasing its speed and harnessing energy. Similarly, the incremental benefits of marginal gains may seem negligible initially. Still, as they accumulate, the momentum grows, eventually leading to significant positive outcomes.

The analogy highlights the idea: consistent efforts in a singular direction, no matter how small, will invariably propel progress. Just as a steady flow of water eventually powers the wheel, consistent incremental improvements can lead to transformative results. It's the age-old logic of cause and effect, much like the mathematical certainty that 2+2=4. Once the right components are in place, and there's consistent effort, the desired outcome becomes not just probable, but predictable.

The Evolution of TLS

In 2022, Traffic and Lighting Systems (TLS Group) celebrated their 40th anniversary. Since their humble inception in 1982, the company weathered various market conditions, as is typical for any venture.

Conventional wisdom posits that business success is measured by yearly milestones. An article from Entrepreneur dated January 3, 2021, titled "The True Failure Rate of Small Business," cites data from the Bureau of Labor Statistics which paints a sobering picture: about 20 percent of small businesses fail within their first year. By the end of a decade, only 30 percent remain operational, pointing to a 70 percent failure rate. Remarkably, 96 percent of contractor companies falter, attributing this to challenges like insufficient cash flow, absence of legal contracts, excessive overhead costs, and a lack of streamlined processes.[110,111]

In 1999, as a second-generation leader, David Willis assumed leadership at TLS Group, steering the company through significant sales milestones, culminating in revenues exceeding $15 million by 2015. As part of an ambitious plan for a new level of success, Larry Butler, then Vice President, stepped in as President to work with Willis for this growth strategy phase.

Together, Willis and Butler began dissecting the business in detail and recognized several areas where friction was most prevalent, and efficiencies could be enhanced. From the list, they focused on what would have the most immediate impact on the day-to-day business and the best ROI. They honed in on one specific area that captured their attention the most: how they quote projects. They then made the decision to invest heavily into this area at whatever the cost. Figuring that if they could remove friction from the quoting process, which at the time could take days and, in some cases, weeks, they would not only increase efficiency, but would also increase exposure to their company through a quick-to-quote process.

They knew in order to build a system that would make the difference, it might require one of the largest investments made until then, outside of construction equipment. The new quoting system investment was $500,000—a bold move for a company with a valuation of $15 million. Two years of development culminated in the 2018 launch of this system and in six months, TLS drastically reduced quote times from days to mere minutes.

This efficiency led to a sales boom, with the company's revenues soaring past $50 million in three years. By 2022, TLS was an attractive acquisition target and was subsequently acquired. TLS found and then executed on marginal gains that, in effect, turned into a much larger opportunity than expected.

TLS's success story punctuates the power of identifying and leveraging marginal gains. Focusing on areas of friction and improving customer service can yield transformative results. When businesses embrace the philosophy of aggregating marginal gains, they can discern which improvements have the most significant impact. Regularly reviewing and fine-tuning these "margins" ensures sustained growth.

Sir David Brailsford's belief that even the simple act of smiling constitutes a marginal gain speaks to the essence of this philosophy. Every controllable aspect, no matter how seemingly trivial, can contribute to greater success over time. By starting with small, incremental improvements, businesses can achieve their desired, predictable outcomes.

Training for Predictable, Scalable, and Repeatable Outcomes

Chick-fil-A sells chicken—they actually sell a lot of chicken. At the time of this writing, compared to Kentucky Fried Chicken's average annual revenue of $1 million per location, Chick-fil-A's average annual revenue per location astonishingly eclipses $6 million, despite being open one day less per week. Chicken is chicken, right? Not necessarily. While both chains offer their unique culinary spin, consumer preference often hinges on more than just the poultry. The overall experience plays a pivotal role. Why does one outpace the other? A superior experience can be even more valuable than the core product itself.[112]

Outcomes don't become predictable by chance. Effective training, which aligns with the company's vision, mission, and values, must be a priority to reduce unpredictability to a minimum.

Here's a stat to digest:

"Continuous training results in 50 percent higher net sales per team member."

HubSpot[113]

Training is arguably one of the absolute ingredients that open the door for successful and predictable outcomes. Not only does it lay the groundwork for predictable outcomes, but it's also critical during the initial stages of a team member's tenure. The first three months often determine cultural fit and potential value addition. Training accelerates this assessment, offering a clear view of the organization's philosophy and setting the stage for mutual growth.

For successful outcomes, it's essential to navigate team members to a point where they amplify value for the company. Continuous training enhances individual contributions, benefiting both the team member and the organization. The emphasis should be on continuous learning, retraining, and alignment with the company's core, structure, and culture. Presenting the core (VMV) , structure, and culture through variations of consistent training will help increase retention, build future leaders of the organization, and grow the customer base much faster than the sink or swim concept—it will produce predictable outcomes across the organization.

Consider this:

"Companies typically spend between $10k and $15k on hiring an individual but allocate merely $2k annually on training."[114]

Poor customer experiences can echo negatively among dissatisfied customers likely sharing their grievances with numerous friends and family. Intriguingly, nine out of ten consumers assert they'd willingly pay more for a superior customer experience.[115]

For consistent outcomes, organizations must root their operations in core values and missions. While sporadic success is possible without these, sustainability becomes questionable. True, enduring success relies on a keen focus on the foundational principles, which in turn fosters repeatable, scalable, and predictable outcomes.

Everyone is in Sales

If you're not growing, you're dying.

Phil Knight

Sales Are a Must

At its root, every business thrives on sales. It's indisputable; sales are the lifeline of a company. And it's paramount for everyone within the organization to grasp this fundamental truth.

Driving a sales mentality throughout the organization and building a strong sales and marketing environment requires, much like everything in Open-Ended Logic, strong dedication to and emphasis on the essentials by asking the "who, what, when, where, how, and why."

Businesses that prioritize and align with a sales-centric approach often reap immediate benefits. Typically, many departments – from IT to accounts payable, customer service to mailrooms – are so engrossed in their specialized functions that the larger sales picture might seem distant. But, by integrating sales training across all departments, every segment starts to link their activities to the primary goal of revenue generation. Consider, for instance, the frequent interactions between accounts receivables and customers.

Too often, sales personnel cringe when accounts payable reaches out to customers over overdue invoices. How many customer defections have been triggered by mismanaged interactions related to invoices, deliveries, or purchase orders? Yet, with proper training, every touchpoint can be transformed from potential conflict to opportunity, solidifying long-term customer relationships.

Statistics underscore the significance of customer service in sales:

- Only 4 percent of dissatisfied customers voice their concerns.
- Loyal customers can be worth up to ten times their initial purchase.
- Selling to existing customers has a 60-70 percent probability of success, compared to 5-20 percent for new prospects.
- An overwhelming 82 percent of consumers have ceased business due to poor customer service.
- Poor customer service has cost companies $75 billion.
- Attracting new customers is six to seven times costlier than retaining current ones.[116,117,118,119,120,121,122,123]

Kristin Smaby, in her book *Being Human is Good Business*, aptly states, "When customers share their stories, they're not just highlighting pain points. They're teaching us how to refine our offerings." The emphasis here is on integrating sales and marketing perspectives across all touchpoints, regardless of the department.[124]

In an era dominated by social media marketing, prioritizing the customer service experience is imperative for long-term sales growth and brand building. When all departments grasp the business's sales dynamics, they gain a comprehensive understanding of customer value in terms of time, social interactions, and financial implications.

When each division understands how the business works fundamentally, from a sales perspective, it gives a broad view of the importance of the customer and how much monetary, social, and time costs are attached to the actual sale.

The most robust companies adopt a holistic sales approach and achieve this by aligning everyone in the organization with the sales and marketing process and training. By driving sales as an internal value-add for customers and the company as a whole, everyone has the ability to become a part of the revenue stream. Team members, when acquainted with their impact on profits and losses, gain a renewed sense of purpose and alignment with the company's broader mission.

Harvey Mackay, author of *Swim with the Sharks Without Being Eaten Alive*, said that when people asked him how many salespeople he had at his envelope company, he said, "500." Then, when asked how many team members he had, he would reply, "500!" This philosophy is mirrored by companies like Zappos, which emphasizes customer service as the cornerstone of sales and long-term profitable growth.[125]

Team members are encouraged to be the absolute best customer service agents and are expected to have conversations with customers averse to the "solve the problems fast and move on to the next customer" model so typically exemplified by other call centers across the world. The fact that Zappos is known for ten-hour conversions is, at first thought, frightening for any owner or manager worried about soft costs; yet this is the very reason Zappos succeeds. Who else receives mainstream press for exemplary service? Zappos understands that each call is a chance to sell future value for buying from Zappos. The process of calling in for a return or another issue is simple. Making the process so fast and easy is the mechanism Zappos uses to encourage sales and stimulate long-term profitable growth.

The notion that each part of the business can turn the average person into a sales machine may be a pipe dream to some. However, to those who can turn all departments into sales generators, it could be the difference between explosive growth and bankruptcy.

For everyone in the organization to be an extension of the sales and/or marketing team is to know the "who, what, when, where, how and why" of the company. Highly successful companies understand and have the forethought to ensure that everyone in the organization can, at the least, answer the following questions.

- What is our vision?
- What is our mission?
- What are our values that we hold true each day and with each action?
- Who are we?
- What do we do?
- Who do we serve?
- Why are we unique to our market and industry?

The question might be, what would happen if everyone in my organization knew the questions above verbatim?

Marc Benioff, the founder of Salesforce, stated that the company cannot own facts, which are products or price, because competitors can always drive down prices and offer similar products. This means that the company can only own two things: its values and unique personality. When people know and, more importantly, understand the purpose of the organization, positive attitudes and increased actions begin to organically gel and take form. This alone distances organizations from their competition and places them higher on the customer's scale of quality service and long-term customer satisfaction.[126]

As Benioff explains in his book *Behind the Cloud*, these extensions will migrate into customers and those customers into partners, and then into a million-member sales team -- a sales army.[127]

The Power of Intelligent Disobedience

Service animals, particularly guide dogs, are meticulously trained to obey the commands of the individuals they assist. However, what's even more intriguing is that a crucial part of their rigorous one- to two-year training involves cultivating the ability to predict potential dangers. These animals must make a nuanced decision: obey their handler's instruction or choose a different course of action when they perceive a threat. This principle, known as intelligent disobedience, stands as one of the most vital components of a service animal's training. The concept may seem counterintuitive — training an animal for obedience, yet also conditioning it to defy a given directive. But this approach has been an integral aspect of service dog training since the 1930s. When faced with danger, the dog evaluates the situation and takes corrective action, even if it goes against the handler's command. At the heart of this is the animal's instinct to prioritize safety, and the handler learns to trust this instinct.

In contrast, many organizations struggle to instill this notion of intelligent disobedience, both from a managerial and a team member standpoint.

The aviation industry provides an alarming example. Several black box recordings from airplane crashes have revealed a lack of transparency and communication. In some of these instances, subordinates withheld critical information or refrained from challenging the decisions of higher-ups, often leading to disastrous results. Their reluctance stemmed from the fear of potential repercussions.

Historical contexts offer further insight. When interrogated about their involvement in atrocities during World War II, some Nazi soldiers justified their actions by claiming they were merely following orders. While it's challenging to accept that such atrocious deeds could be solely based on directives, it compels us to reflect on how continuous conditioning can profoundly warp judgment. How often, in less extreme contexts, do individuals suppress their concerns or hesitate to challenge superiors due to an intimidating environment? How frequently is irrationality tolerated because of societal or organizational pressures?

For organizations to thrive, fostering a culture that encourages transparency and intelligent disobedience is crucial. A value-driven environment allows individuals to express their concerns openly and prevents moral dilemmas that might lead to adverse outcomes.[128]

The Milgram Shock Experiment: Lessons for Organizations

In 1961, not long after Adolf Eichmann's trial for Nazi war crimes, psychologist Stanley Milgram initiated a groundbreaking study at Yale University. He aimed to test human obedience to authority figures against individual conscience.

The experiment was conducted in two adjacent rooms on the Yale campus. One room held two individuals, the "Examiner" overseeing the experiment and the "Teacher," a paid volunteer. The second room housed the "Learner," an actor pretending to be another participant. Unknown to the Teacher, "the real" test subject, the actual experiment revolved around them. The ad that promoted the experiment stated that volunteers would receive $4 for one hour, worth $33 today.

The Teacher was led to believe that the study was evaluating the Learner's memory. For every mistake the Learner made, the Teacher was to administer an escalating electric shock. The Teacher was told the electric shocks would be increased in increments of 15 volts for each wrong answer, up to a maximum of 450 volts. While no actual shocks were given, the actor convincingly portrayed pain with every increase in voltage.

The shock levels were labeled for the Teacher: Slight Shock, Moderate Shock, Strong Shock, Very Strong Shock, Intense Shock, Extreme Intensity Shock, Danger: Severe Shock, and XXX, meaning potential death. When the Teacher showed any sign of resistance to administering a shock, the Examiner would say the following script, in this order:

1. "Please continue."
2. "The experiment requires that you continue."
3. "It is absolutely essential that you continue."
4. "You have no other choice; you must go on."

If the Teacher refused to continue even after the fourth demand, the experiment would be paused. The experiment was finished after three paused sessions. Despite increasing discomfort, when Teachers hesitated to continue, the Examiner would prompt them to go on. Surprisingly, a large percentage of participants complied, even when they believed they might be causing serious harm.

The results were that out of forty volunteers, roughly 62 percent administered all levels of shocks, and the other 35 to 38 percent held off on administering the final shock, although it is noted that they came close in some cases. The conclusion was that people obeyed instructions based on authority. In this case, the Examiner was wearing a lab coat to illustrate authority.[129]

The study revealed two main insights:

- **The Power of Authority:** Individuals often succumb to authoritative figures, even when morally conflicted. In this experiment, the simple attire of a lab coat swayed participants, indicating that symbols and trappings of authority can have a potent influence.
- **The Danger of Silence:** A failure to voice concerns, challenge dubious commands, or disobey can lead to dire consequences.

This is best illustrated by Volkswagen, which became the center of attention in 2015 when it was revealed that engineers buckled to upper-level management's initiative to produce false claims about miles per gallon and environmental benefits. It was Milgram's Shock Experiment all over again, but in this case involving real people, with real implications and real costs. Volkswagen's cost was not only a $20 billion blunder but left a corporate stain of poor values witnessed across the world. Irrational behavior can deteriorate rational logic inch by inch.[130]

But how can organizations insulate themselves from these pitfalls? The answer lies in embracing transparency and cultivating an environment where questioning and constructive criticism are not just accepted but actively encouraged. This is what Ray Dalio, the founder of Bridgewater Associates, refers to as "radical transparency." He believes that an organization's success hinges on its ability to foster open, honest dialogues, regardless of hierarchy.[131]

The Milgram experiment serves as a stark reminder of human fallibility, especially when under the influence of authority. By understanding and acknowledging this, organizations can actively work towards creating a culture that values ethics over obedience.[132]

"It's Just Peanut Butter"

The Peanut Corporation of America (PCA) started in 1977 in Lynchburg, Virginia, as a family-run venture by Hugh Parnell. While it changed hands in 1995, the Parnell brothers remained connected to PCA, with Steward eventually reclaiming ownership in 2000.

From the 1980s, cleanliness and quality standards at PCA were questionable. Despite frequent alerts from the FDA and uneasy customers, the corporation continually dismissed concerns. One particularly alarming record showed PCA failing 40 out of 40 FDA standards. Despite these glaring issues, management continued their operations as they always had.

In one of PCA's last instances, a team member raised an alarm by sending a memo stating that they needed to stop production and halt shipments due to certain batches of peanut butter being contaminated with mold and mouse droppings. Refusing to address these serious concerns by making a customer-centric decision, Steward Parnell chose to proceed with shipments and focus on revenue versus loss. The consequences were devastating. More than 700 individuals, including children, were infected, with nine instances where food poisoning was a factor in the deaths. Parnell is now serving a 28-year sentence in federal prison for that decision. But was it solely because of that decision? It began with a choice made years earlier to overlook an incident. This negligence grew as more prominent and evident issues arose. In retrospect, it might have been that initial oversight with the FDA, coupled with not prioritizing their customers' health, that led to this outcome.[133]

It's worth noting that the term "intelligent disobedience" might be misinterpreted due to its negative connotations. Perhaps a more apt phrase might be "intelligent transparency." Organizations must encourage an environment where openness is celebrated and where their vision, mission, and values serve as touchstones for daily operations. This proactive approach can significantly reduce bureaucratic barriers and foster an organic, successful growth pattern.

The downfall of PCA is no different than scandals such as those faced by GMC, Volkswagen, Western Union, and a litany of others. These examples punctuate the necessity of processes that encourage intelligent transparency, much like what Ray Dalio has established at Bridgewater Associates. Regardless of the industry—be it automotive, tech, insurance, entertainment, food, or finance—a lack of systems to identify and rectify issues is a ticking time bomb. Without a commitment to transparent operations and values-driven decision-making, organizations risk monumental setbacks, both in reputation and operation.

The Power of Preparation

The meticulousness of an organization's planning quickly becomes evident during the execution of an event or outcome. Without a doubt, achieving long-term profitable growth centers on comprehensive preparation, stretching from the highest echelons to the grassroots level. Peter Drucker famously remarked, "Execution eats strategy for lunch." At the heart of impeccable execution lies thorough preparation. Whether it's a classroom lecture or a boardroom presentation, addressing the fundamental questions - "who, what, when, where, how, and why" - is essential for effective preparation and delivery.

Organizations deep-seated in Open-Ended Logic emphasize consistent preparation, cultivating a culture that strives for clear, tangible outcomes. The more an organization, team, or individual prepares, the more accurately they can predict and reach their desired destination.

With brutal preparation we also become more courageous to drive our missions, confronting the fear of obstacles ahead.[134]

Churchill: Mastering the Art of Preparation

Winston Churchill, the iconic British leader, had an extraordinary gift for transforming simple phrases into timeless oratorical treasures. As a child, Churchill grappled with a stutter, a lisp, and an inherent shyness. Yet, he tenaciously battled these challenges and emerged as a beacon of oratory excellence. His influence didn't stop there; he was also celebrated for his power to unify allies and nations, especially during times of conflict and strife. One of Churchill's remarkable rhetorical tools was his adept use of chiasmus, or the inversion of word order in parallel phrases.[135]

Some renowned examples of Churchill's chiasmi include:

- "I am ready to meet my maker; whether my maker is ready for the great ordeal of meeting me is another question."
- "We shape our buildings and afterwards our buildings shape us."
- "Now this is not the end. It is not even the beginning of the end. But it is, perhaps, the end of the beginning."

Churchill's eloquence often appeared effortless. Still, behind the scenes, he dedicated hours to meticulous preparation for his speeches. For instance, a ten-minute address required a week of preparation, while a forty-minute one could demand six to eight hours just for the initial draft. He poured in this effort because he wanted his words to etch a lasting impression on his listeners. He aimed to craft what Ryan Holiday, in his book *Perennial Sellers*, terms an "indefinite and enduring moment in time."

Perennial – something that persists; enduring, recurrent, and infinite in nature.[136]

Holiday argues that genuine masterpieces, be it art, literature, or technology, emerge from sustained effort, resilience, and above all, preparation. What distinguishes a perennial success? It is the ability to produce work that stands the test of time and resonates for years to come. True quality emerges when minute, intricate details are woven together with careful thought and commitment. Such depth and complexity are not just confined to artistic endeavors but are also pivotal in the business landscape through gestures and experiences.[137]

Consistently, certain teams and organizations eclipse others in terms of performance and innovation. But what causes some giants to stumble while upstarts soar to greatness? The key is often meticulous preparation translating into lasting relevance. Companies must critically ask themselves: Do we genuinely understand our customer's needs? How can we remain forefront in our consumer's minds? What sets us apart and makes us scalable? How close are we to realizing our vision, and is our mission aligned?

In essence, true preparation equips organizations for enduring success and foresight. It's not just about readying oneself for the present, but also for perennial relevance in the future.

The Organizational Role of Risk

Imagine a world where the fear of failure was non-existent. Would you be bolder in your career moves, stake everything you have, or demand more from yourself, your life, and your organization? Would you push your boundaries to their utmost limits? Fundamentally, if the risk of failure wasn't looming over us, wouldn't our appetite for risk be significantly heightened? Many of the organizations and individuals discussed in this book have woven tales of resilience, determination, and risk-taking.

Risk and failure often go hand in hand. As organizations scale, achieving financial stability, customer loyalty, and market position, there's a tendency to de-emphasize the very risk-taking that contributed to their success. The very risks that were once celebrated become viewed as missteps or actions they wouldn't replicate. Although financial stability is vital, it doesn't guarantee future success. Often, it's in moments of struggle and adversity that we're more inclined to take risks, to innovate, and to push boundaries.

There's a danger in becoming too complacent or overly reliant on past achievements. While financial security is the lifeblood of a business, avoiding risks can lead to stagnation. Consider Warren Buffet, often lauded for his conservative investments. Yet, it was he who took a substantial calculated risk by doubling down on American Express in 1963, during a tumultuous period for the company. This audacious move solidified a monumental trajectory for Berkshire Hathaway.

Similarly, Amazon's continued ascent can be attributed to its relentless "Day-One" mentality, which emphasizes continuous innovation and the mindset of always being the underdog. This approach serves as a cautionary tale against resting on past laurels. Past market leaders like Kmart, Sears, and BlackBerry witnessed their decline, largely due to an overreliance on their previous successes.

Removing risk from an organization's strategy or lexicon could be a red flag. To evolve and grow, revisiting past strategies and determining future directions becomes crucial. How do we strike a balance between being cautious and taking calculated risks? Embracing risk, albeit in a measured way, is essential for innovation and progress. It's imperative to understand and respect risk, ensuring it remains a part of an organization's toolkit. Keep risk around and remind the organization that it'll always have a room in the house.[138]

Conclusion: Embracing Structure

The backbone of any organization is its structure – a robust framework that requires regular nurturing, constant evolution, and sometimes, even reinvention. It's this structure that we test, challenge, and push to its limits, both as individual contributors and as a collective unit – a team.

Structure isn't about rigidity or endurance. Instead, it's about adaptability and resilience. Just as life is punctuated by successes and setbacks, an organization's journey is marked by achievements and obstacles. Through each misstep, we gain invaluable insights. We become more tenacious, more prepared, and more alert to the challenges ahead.

Reflecting on Edison's persistence with the lightbulb, it reminds us that true innovation often comes after repeated attempts, after countless iterations. And when the breakthrough finally happens, it doesn't just illuminate our path, it lights our world, setting a precedent and paving the way for further discovery.

So, as we contemplate the structure of our organizations, let's view it not as a constraint, but as a catalyst – a dynamic platform that fosters innovation, nurtures talent, and propels us towards new horizons. Let's find those poised and waiting for an opportunity to shine and be part of something incredible – a remarkable journey.

PART 3: CULTURE / THE RIM

PURPOSE

COLLABORATION

ENGAGEMENT

IMPERMEABLE RELATIONSHIPS

VIBE

APPRECIATION

PERSISTENCE

PEOPLE

A Culture of Purpose

Purpose – the reason for which something exists or is done, made, used, etc.[139]

On August 17, 2017, Hurricane Harvey was charting a direct path towards Corpus Christi. However, it made its ferocious landfall near Rockport, Texas, a mere 32 miles from Corpus Christi, intensifying into a Category 4 hurricane with winds gusting up to 130 mph. In a matter of hours, Harvey inundated Texas and parts of southwest Louisiana with an astonishing fifty-two inches of rain. Houston bore the brunt of its rage, setting an all-time continental U.S. Tropical cyclone record. The deluge transformed the city into an urban lake over its concrete mass, leaving most of its residents to seek shelter within the 24 hours.

In this bleak scenario, Gallery Furniture emerged as a shining light of hope. With three stores in the Houston area, the company promptly threw open its doors to the stranded. Under the leadership of Founder and CEO, Jim McIngvale, no one seeking refuge was turned away. Remarkably, two of its three stores sheltered a combined total of 800 people. McIngvale didn't just provide housing for a day or for the week Hurricane Harvey hovered over Houston—he opened the doors indefinitely.

McIngvale's business philosophy is centered around community welfare. He firmly believes, "We all have a responsibility for the well-being of our community. That's the central theme of our culture here. We know that if we help these citizens when they're in need, they will help us." When posed with a choice, "Are you going to be a shelter or a furniture store?" McIngvale replied, "There's no reason we can't be both."[140,141]

Tough Mudder's Genesis

In 2010, venturing into the muddy terrains of challenging sports events, Will Dean, founder and CEO of Tough Mudder, set out on what many perceived as a wild and impossible endeavor. As mentioned earlier, Dean's innovation revolved around mud, carving out a niche for enthusiasts who sought a unique physical challenge. Dean's book, *It Takes a Tribe*, chronicles the inception of Tough Mudder in Allentown, Pennsylvania. In shaping the culture of the enterprise, Dean, in collaboration with the then-COO Guy Livingstone, envisioned a defining pledge for participants.

The Tough Mudder pledge embodies:

- I understand that Tough Mudder is not a race but a challenge
- I put teamwork and camaraderie before my course time
- I do not whine – kids whine
- I help my fellow Mudder complete the course
- I overcome all fears

This pledge could well resonate with many organizations; It's, well, tough! Dean wanted to create something that would stand out but also give a team environment and not make anyone think that this was about "time." Typically, we're all governed by time - the clock - and how far we can get ahead of the next person, whether friend or foe. Tough Mudder's premise is to ensure everyone understands they're on the same playing field— that if you're competing in the Tough Mudder, you're only competing against yourself. This is the day you take on your fear and you conquer it. The Mudder spirit hinges on collective achievement, ensuring every Mudder crosses the finish line.

This very spirit permeates the organizational culture of Tough Mudder. Aptly termed as the TMHQ PACT, it encapsulates the principles of Pride, Accountability, Continuous Improvement, and Teamwork. These principles not only define team member interactions but also influence the brand's engagement with its customers and teammates.

The Tough Mudder organization operates on the terms of this pact.[142]

Pride:

- Accept only the best
- Demonstrate integrity at all times
- Constantly delight our customers

Accountability:

- Focus on outcomes, not inputs
- Treat the company's money like our own
- Deliver on our promises

Continuous Improvement:

- View problems as opportunities
- Drive innovation and embrace change
- Accept feedback and learn from mistakes

Teamwork:

- Build lasting relationships
- Never say "that's not my job"
- Don't let each other fail

With over ten thousand participants on average at each event and a global community of over six million veterans from around the world, Tough Mudder continues to make its way up and down the muddy mountains and valleys of rigid terrain to emerge the leader in an industry surrounded by mud.

HubSpot

Here's HubSpot's perspective on how culture propels purpose: they have crafted ten culture code points that align with their mission. Any company's mission can serve as an incredible force that pushes a richer culture for current and future generations.

HubSpot's 10 Culture Code Points

1. We are as maniacal about our metrics as our mission.
2. We obsess over customers, not competitors.
3. We are radically and uncomfortably transparent.
4. We give ourselves the autonomy to be awesome.
5. We are unreasonably selective about our peers.
6. We invest in individual mastery and market value.
7. We defy conventional "wisdom" as it's often unwise.
8. We speak the truth and face the facts.
9. We believe in work + life, not work vs. life.
10. We are a perpetual work in progress.

HubSpot Employee Alignment

HubSpot's mission, vision, and values motivate 95 percent of HubSpot employees. Besides getting paid, the "company mission" is the most important thing about their work for 23 percent of employees at HubSpot. 26 percent of employees say that the main reason they stay at HubSpot is because of the HubSpot company mission. When asked to whom they feel the most loyal at work, 25 percent of employees said HubSpot's mission and vision. Comparably data clearly shows that a focused mission statement and cohesive core company values are vital to maintaining employee alignment.[143]

Open-Ended Culture

The fact is that the system that people work in and the interaction with people may account for 90- or 95 percent of performance.

W. Edward Fleming

Open-Ended Culture

Culture is the foundational perspective within an organization, guiding the team towards the vision, mission, and values. The culture of a company can propel it to success or lead it to its demise.

Take the case of Apple. When John Sculley took the reins, Apple's innovative and open-minded psyche began to shift. It wasn't immediate, but Apple quickly experienced culture shock with the exit of Steve Jobs. Apple started as a hub of creativity and open mindedness and fell into a process-driven organization of suits and ties, dissolving into a mindset of blocks with straight lines and pointy corners. The culture changed and so did the vision and mission in the mind of Apple, the artists and team members of Apple, and then, in the mind of the consumer.

In Al Ries and Jack Trout's book, *Positioning*, the idea is presented that owning the mind of the customer (within an industry's prospective market) is the central point of an organization's marketing goal, yet we fail to understand that positioning begins in the mind of the team member first. It then transcends through the team member attitude toward the mind of the customer. The position of any team member's mind toward company culture can be described as Belief, Action, Stagnant, or Non-Committal.[144]

With Jobs at the helm, Apple was moving in the direction of being a great company, but it lost the flavor when he was let go. It might have helped a little in the beginning if Sculley had walked in with jeans and flip flops the day after Jobs departed. However, without authenticity it would have invariably failed. The reality – Apple's culture changed. Apple was knocked off course from its vision and mission, going from a creative tech company to a traditional computer brand even though products like Apple Newton emerged. Different industries require different thought processes and doses of illogical and irrational intuitiveness -- the intangible. Sculley wasn't the guy Jobs was, but without the jolt of being forced out, Jobs more than likely wouldn't have been prepared to operate from a different point of view. The fact — Apple needed the visionary, and Jobs re-emerged with a vengeance.

The culture at Fairchild Semiconductors in the 50s was a complete turnaround from Shockley Semiconductors. Noyce's leadership at Fairchild Semiconductors exemplifies the significance of a positive culture. His encouragement as people would exit his cubicle, or gatherings, was to... "Go do something wonderful" – it fostered a culture of innovation, risk-taking, and accomplishment.

Disney, under the helm of Walt Disney, nurtured a culture of imagination, constantly pushing the boundaries of technology and creativity. They developed new technology with every new animated movie and then theme park. Disney continued to try new things and take new risks to find what stuck and drove more inventive ways to entertain and make people happy.

At Walmart's helm, Sam Walton's leadership approach was to give store managers significant autonomy, empowering them to innovate. An illustrative example comes from one of the early Walmart stores. A manager, in anticipation of a grand opening, purchased truckloads of watermelons. However, during a particularly hot summer day, with small parking lots forcing many customers to park in adjacent fields, the heat caused the watermelons to burst. The result was a chaotic scene both inside and outside the store, with burst watermelons everywhere. Yet, instead of reprimanding the manager, Walton commended him and said it was a risk worth taking. Walton believed that risks, even if they didn't always pay off, were integral to innovation. His decision to entrust store managers with significant responsibility played a pivotal role in Walmart's success. This freedom to ideate and implement, even if it meant occasional failures, fostered a culture where risks were seen as opportunities for learning and growth.[145]

Similarly, Zappos isn't merely a shoe retailer; its culture prioritizes unparalleled customer service, valuing the bond created with customers. They have the task of being "the problem solver" who puts into action steps to fix customer issues. Stay on the phone, solve people's problems, entertain, and create an advocate from thousands of miles away. Zappos isn't selling shoes; they're selling a trusted service with peace of mind.

These cultures have grown beyond expectations and continue to thrive. And although some of these now-behemoth companies have grown into process-generating organizations, at the heart, professional autonomy is still loud and clear.

A Culture of Contribution

You can't motivate people. That door is locked from the inside. You CAN create a climate in which most of your people will motivate themselves to help the company reach its objectives.

Robert Townsend (Avis CEO)

Dorman Products stands as a testament to innovation within the automotive and heavy-duty truck aftermarket industry. Established in 1918, the company originally produced nuts and bolts. However, as the years rolled on, Dorman evolved, capitalizing on the expiration of original equipment manufacturer (OEM) patents by re-engineering and manufacturing those parts.

Today, their dynamic corporate culture pulsates with energy and innovation. Their expansive million-square-foot facility in Philadelphia is a hub of R&D activities. Unlike the traditional siloed workspace, engineers work side by side on the assembly floor, and even patent attorneys, rather than being confined to closed offices, utilize open desks and cubicles. This facilitates constant interaction, discussion, and exchange of ideas, encouraging a culture of collaborative innovation.

In 1971, brothers Richard and Steven Berman confronted declining sales with a proactive approach: they sought direct feedback from their customers. Their inquiry was straightforward: "What do you need, and how can we assist?" This led them to a mechanic who highlighted the difficulty in procuring replacement window handles. Upon discovering that the OEM charged an exorbitant $50 per handle, the Bermans recognized a golden opportunity. Capitalizing on this insight, they reshaped their business model, propelling their venture into a billion-dollar publicly traded company.

In the formative phase of their re-engineering journey, Dorman recognized the necessity of shattering conventional barriers to keep pace in the rapidly evolving automotive aftermarket industry. Collaboration was crucial, linking the efforts of engineering to sales, marketing, and distribution. This collective contribution not only reduced costs and enhanced efficiency but also instilled a sense of entrepreneurship among team members, fostering a unifying "we can do it together" mindset.

At Dorman, every team member is referred to as a "Contributor." This designation reinforces Dorman's philosophy that, regardless of one's role or designation, each individual is a valued Contributor, bringing their distinct ideas and skills to the organization's strategies, operations, and decisions.

Doorman's website says:

> *At our heart, we do two things: supply new products that match the fit, function and performance of original equipment manufacturer parts, and reengineer parts to fix common flaws in original part designs. Our talented team is constantly evaluating what parts are failing on today's vehicles, so that we can steadily deliver reliable replacements.*
>
> *We accomplish this through our Culture of Contribution. Our employees are called Contributors because we genuinely value every new idea our people contribute. This collaborative, entrepreneurial spirit is what drives the thousands of new products we release every year.*[146]

Culture of Action

Action – the process or state of acting or being active.[147]

When you engage with Grant Cardone, whether it's through reading one of his books, listening to his podcast, or watching his 10x features, it's almost certain you'll leave feeling invigorated. Cardone's dynamic energy stems from his compelling drive for action. He ranks among the top business magnates primarily because he consistently pushes limits with his unbridled passion and holds elevated expectations in every aspect — from personal life to family and business. As he remarked on CNBC Make It in February 2018, "I'm wealthy because I have courage, creativity, and commitment."

Action creates Energy

Cardone's *The 10X Rule* emphasizes not just amplifying one's goals but adopting audacious aspirations and backing them with deliberate action. The book's core idea is straightforward: if, as a salesperson, you plan on calling ten people in a day and hope for outstanding results, you might want to recalibrate your approach. Instead, the 10X mindset would have you reach out to a hundred people, actively driving those audacious outcomes. Cardone emphasizes that discomfort and challenges are part and parcel of the journey. Taking proactive steps helps you overcome periods of disheartenment and skepticism, steering you towards unparalleled achievements. And he doesn't just preach this philosophy — he embodies it. Every day, he's on a mission to touch the lives of over six billion people in his lifetime, demonstrated by his unyielding dedication to vlogging on platforms like Instagram, Facebook, YouTube, TikTok, and other social media outlets.

"Never lower your target; increase your actions."

The 10x Rule

Grant Cardone[148]

Action is not just a trait embodied by Cardone but is deeply embedded in the DNA of his entire organization. This action-oriented mindset is infectious, pulsating through every facet of the various businesses he oversees. His empire, estimated to be worth around $5 billion, spans a range of ventures including Cardone Training Technologies, Cardone University, Cardone Acquisitions, Cardone Capital, and the Grant Cardone TV Network. Cardone believes in four distinct levels of action: (1) Do Nothing; (2) Retreat; (3) Normal levels of Action; and (4) Massive Action. He contends that once you commit to the fourth level – massive action – there's a fundamental shift in mindset, leading to transformative results.[149]

Cardone stands out as a torch of leadership, achieving success through his commitment to action and an undeniable obsession for his mission.[150]

Culture of Leadership

In 1970, Robert Greenleaf penned an essay that stirred the management sector. Greenleaf's essay was entitled "The Servant as Leader" and consisted of servanthood tools including listening, persuasion, access to intuition and foresight, use of language, and pragmatic measurements of outcomes.

The concept of Servant Leadership took root during Greenleaf's tenure at AT&T, where he disseminated his philosophy over his three-and-a-half-decade managerial stint. He once remarked that his aspiration to exercise "was to have a career of quiet influence." While Greenleaf's impact was hardly quiet, his leadership principles were undeniable, leading him to spearhead the company's first management training program. Through his observations, he discerned a distinct leadership style exhibited by the heads of AT&T's most successful units. These leaders behaved more like nurturing coaches, showing equal concern for both the organization and its team members. They prioritized serving the needs of their teams and believed in the cohesive relationship between an individual and the organization. As Greenleaf aptly put it, "the organization exists for the person as much as the person exists for the organization."[151]

Servant leadership has gained significant traction in contemporary business circles, with many organizations embracing this approach and reaping tangible benefits. In this leadership style, leaders prioritize serving their teams and groups, flipping traditional leadership dynamics, and placing emphasis on the needs and growth of team members.

Servant – one that serves others.

Leadership – the position or function of a leader, a person who guides or directs a group.[152,153]

The term 'servant leadership' might seem paradoxical at first glance, combining two seemingly contradictory terms. At its core, it summarizes the philosophy of "leading by serving." When fully realized, this leadership model embodies characteristics such as active listening, empathy, healing, self-awareness, forward-thinking, stewardship, and a genuine commitment to the growth and well-being of individuals. As a result, those at the frontline, often closest to the consumer, also mirror these attributes, ensuring that the principles of servant leadership touch every facet of the organization.

Numerous organizations today have embraced servant leadership, including renowned names like Starbucks, QuickTrip, Zappos, Nordstrom, Vanderbilt University, Southwest Airlines, ServiceMaster, and St. Joseph Regional Medical Center. Notably, even branches of the United States military, including the Air Force, Army, Marine Corps, and Navy, have integrated these values. When an organization prioritizes servanthood, its vision not only becomes more attainable but also gains the trust and commitment of its stakeholders.

myTime

Aron Ain, the CEO of UKG and former head of Kronos, has played a pivotal role in revolutionizing workplace management software and services. Post his graduation from Hamilton College in 1979, Ain climbed the corporate ladder at Kronos, holding various positions over his four-decade tenure. In 2016, aiming for greater transparency within the company, Ain introduced the "myTime" concept for U.S. operations. This groundbreaking idea essentially redefined traditional "vacation days" under his "Family First" initiative. Such a commitment to prioritizing family is rare in the modern corporate landscape, particularly from a CEO overseeing a $1.4-billion enterprise.

Ain said, "I constantly tell people that if their job or career is the most important thing in their life – the activity they care most about and invest the most in – they're making a profound and tragic mistake." He lives this outlook by leaving work on a Wednesday at 2pm to watch his kids play sports. His philosophy is that if you hire the right people who have the talent and work ethic, they will get the job done.[154]

Even though Kronos's average vacation time grew by 2.6 days from 2015 to 2016, Ain credits the plan for record profits in 2016. Engagement rose from 84 percent to 87 percent, and turnover dropped from 6.4 percent to 5.6 percent in one year. When you factor in that Kronos had a team member base of over four thousand people at the time (now six thousand), these are large numbers. Ain is a two-time winner of Glassdoor's Highest Rated CEO award as well as the Ray Stata Leadership and Innovation Award. Mass Technology Council named him CEO of the Year, and Ernst & Young honored him as Entrepreneur of the Year. Additionally, Ain was profiled in The New York Times in an article about "The Incalculable Value of a Good Boss."

On the podcast "Lessons in Leadership," Adam Mendler asked Ain, "What is the best advice you have on building, managing, and leading teams?"[155] Ain answered, "Put your ego aside. Make it about the team, not you. Trust your people, and don't micromanage. Don't get hung up on your own authority and title. Don't feel you always have to be right. And for goodness sake, have fun! Why does work always have to be so serious?"

Servant leadership comes in the form of many different initiatives that encompass the team member and organization. Leadership is serving. Serving is identifying where we can help each other become successful to make the organization as a whole flourish. Central to our approach is bridging departmental divides. Initiating this within the framework of servant leadership paves the way for organizational alignment. Embracing collaboration should be the norm, not the exception.

By serving others, individuals quickly recognize the extensive benefits, reaping rewards for themselves. These actions embed a deep sense of purpose, aligning the organization with its vision. Prioritize a service-oriented mindset in your team and reap the rewards in performance and culture.

Culture of Grit & Persistence

Grit – firmness of character; indomitable spirit; pluck (dictionary.com)

Persistence – the continuance of an effect after the cause of it has stopped; persistence of vision (dictionary.com)

Jack Ma, Alibaba founder and chairman, doesn't look for the top-of-class candidates when hiring. He looks for the right people for Alibaba, and he knows what that individual looks like—how they will mesh with the team and produce results. Ma generally seeks out those who are number two or three in their class. He believes they'll have something to prove. Angela Duckworth describes this attribute as grit in her book subsequently titled - *Grit*.

Grit and persistence, while often used interchangeably, have subtle differences. Persistence speaks to an inner drive that keeps one moving forward, but grit takes it a step further. Grit isn't just about having that drive, but actively harnessing and acting upon that tenacity. It embodies a relentless, unyielding attitude.

When researching successful organizations, groups, and teams, and their leadership, it's not hard to connect the dots. None of our examples throughout Open-Ended Logic had easy streets laid in front of them, and it's safe to say the people behind these companies had many hurdles to overcome. Disney lost Oswald, Noyce was part of the "Traitorous Eight," Jobs was fired from the company he founded out of his garage, Cardone started from scratch and lost practically everything in 2008, and Bezos continued to battle major financial struggles from skyrocket growth. The unifying thread in these success stories? A true sense of grit and persistence.

When an organization is infused with grit and persistence, limitless growth becomes a genuine possibility. Take Zappos, for instance: they empower their customer service representatives to independently address issues to enhance customer satisfaction. Similarly, Disney's CEO Bob Iger encourages teams to take calculated risks to elevate the companies under his leadership.

The freedom to make mistakes for the better of the organization allows grit and persistence to steer the organization. If you think about it, Open–Ended Logic organizations inspire their people to embrace and execute persistence. This applies not only for the sales team but for accounting, customer service, facilities maintenance, and all the way to the frontline. We all have a duty to do what we can to help the company succeed through grit and persistence.

In essence, we're compensated to embody grit and persistence in our quest for consistent excellence. This call is bequeathed to us, and we now have the freedom to excel. There is no excuse. We must do our best to pave the path to success.[156]

Impermeable Relationships

Two are better than one, because they have a good return for their labor: If either of them falls down, one can help the other up.

Ecclesiastes 4:9-10

From the Cadbury brothers working together in pursuit of better chocolate and team member safety, to Michael Eisner and Frank Wells seizing control of Disney, to Phil Knight and his group of "Buttfaces," relationships remain the little BIG thing that can define success or cause downfall. In The Man Behind the Microchip, Leslie Berlin describes the relationships of the Fairchild Semiconductor team (aka the "Traitorous Eight") by stating, "The rapport the eight of them shared was dynamic and impermeable."

Berlin sums up this description of impermeable rapport with the following paragraph:

> *They often found themselves standing in a circle when they were together, their shoulders nearly touching, each man holding one conversation with the man on his left and a different one with the man on his right (and perhaps a third with someone across the circle). Noyce loved these moments, loved the buzz of talk and the smell of cigarettes many of them held between their lips. If he reached in his pocket for a smoke and discovered an empty pack, he would crumple the wrapper, toss it on the ground, grab a cigarette out of his neighbor's pocket (without asking and almost without looking), pound it*

> *on his leg, and pop it in his mouth so the guy from whom he took it could light it. Were it filtered, Noyce would grumble something about sissies. All the while, he and the other fellows would maintain their end of the two or three conversations.*[157]

This description gives an articulate and surreal view of how the men worked with each other at Fairchild Semiconductor in the 1950s and '60s—how they interacted with and trusted each other. Almost to the point of empirical evidence, we know that having an impermeable relationship strengthens the core, thus creating an impenetrable relationship of complete trust that speaks to the fact that, "We're in this together, I've got your back, and I know you have mine." What a sensation it creates throughout the organization when trust is a fundamental cornerstone.

Generally, relationships latch on elements like time spent together, social capital with an individual, common interests, and deep-rooted bonds like family ties or marital commitments. These qualities build pathways to trust. Yet, when Bob Noyce and Gordon Moore left Fairchild Semiconductors to establish Intel on July 8, 1968, their dynamic defied this norm. In fact, they didn't visit much, didn't have the same interests, and they certainly didn't share the same social experiences outside of work. They were actually quite the opposite. While Bob never tired of finding the next "gathering" to partake in, Gordon was happy being behind the scenes, reserved and quiet. Despite their differences, they collaborated seamlessly, shared profound mutual respect. They possessed a bond—an impermeable relationship.

The Pragmatist & The Dreamer

"Absolutely not" was a common reply Walt Disney heard through his many years working with Roy Disney, his brother, friend, and business partner. One of the most interesting facts about the business relationship between Walt and Roy is that although they argued and disagreed on future plans a lot, they had an immeasurable trust in each other. Disneyland was an idea Walt had at the time of Snow White's creation, and for well over ten years, the idea grew. Walt kept quiet and studied, learned, and watched, developing the idea into the future vision that made it the next big thing in the '50s for Disney Productions.

Since the inception of Disney Productions, Walt had always understood the dynamics of his partnership with his brother, Roy. To gain Roy's support, Walt knew he had to prepare and present a well-thought-out vision, demonstrating commitment to make seemingly unattainable dreams achievable. Whenever Roy voiced doubts, Walt would persistently push his ideas, with even more vigor, until he gained Roy's approval. While Roy was the practical thinker, Walt was the visionary who backed his dreams with action. Their unique dynamic proved beneficial for both. As biographer Neal Gabler aptly noted on Roy, "He got joy out of participating in the kind of wild schemes of his brother that he himself would never have concocted.... Roy got release and Walt got protection."[158]

While Walt was the creative genius, Roy put structure and foundational processes in place to allow this creativity to flow. This dynamic highlighted Roy's unique ability to amplify Walt's talents. Roy made Walt better due to the impermeable relationship they had. The trend of failure surrounded Walt like a capsule until Roy joined Walt as a partner in Disney Productions. At the time of moving studios in 1926, Walt, alone, decided to change the studio name from Disney Brothers Studio to Walt Disney Studio. Roy accepted without complaint. Historian Steven Watts said, "Walt Disney believed that it was his vision of creativity and entertainment that was the engine of this enterprise and that's what was being sold." Roy agreed and supported him by being the foundation Walt needed for both to succeed. Authentic partnerships are built on profound trust and loyalty, ingredients essential to forging impermeable relationships.[159]

Impermeable relationships do not require a biological relationship, as in the Disney brothers' case, and biology doesn't guarantee an enduring relationship. While they shared a familial bond, their relationship was punctuated by disagreements. In one instance, they had a falling out that lasted between one and two years, only to be mended when Walt extended an olive branch in the form of a peace pipe, signaling his desire for reconciliation.

Similarly, the synergy between Steve Jobs and Steve "Woz" Wozniak was undeniable. While both could be described as "brilliant" in their own right, their combined strengths amplified their individual brilliance. Jobs' visionary approach complemented Woz's technical prowess. Conversely, Woz's creations were elevated by Jobs' insistence on revolutionary design and market viability. Together, they brought the world the Macintosh, becoming a game-changer in the tech industry.

Jobs and Woz shared a unique, unbreakable bond, whereas the relationship between Jobs and John Sculley was fragile. At that juncture in his life, Jobs wasn't particularly inclined to form close ties with another visionary and strong-willed creative. He meshed better with individuals like Woz, who looked to Jobs for artistic direction, business acumen, and assertive decision-making. Authentic relationships, rooted in mutual respect and understanding, naturally evolve into deeper, more cohesive bonds. Relationships that are artificially constructed or forced seldom succeed. Bob Noyce and Gordon Moore might have had distinct personal interests outside of Intel, but their shared vision for the company's future and its role in the evolution of transistors was in perfect sync. Their common objectives and aligned values made for a formidable partnership.

Who is your muse? Are you spending time with them enough and cultivating the relationship to better you, your team and organization?

These instances illustrate that the backbone of a business's success and steady expansion is firmly established in resilient relationships from the highest ranks to the foundational levels, spanning every corner and facet. But who influences whom? Often, our greatest inspirations come from those either mirroring our qualities or starkly contrasting them, challenging our perspectives, and enhancing our capabilities.

Unyielding relationships foster a seamless synergy and inner tenacity that align towards a shared mission and vision.

Winning with Impermeable Relationships

After Villanova's Final Four national title win in 2018, Martha MacCallum, on her Fox News show The Story, asked Rev. Robert Hagan, Villanova Associate Athletic Director and team chaplain, "What is the secret to your success?" He replied:

> *"A lot of people have been asking that, and they are very talented and gifted. They know how to play. But what they really have is togetherness – they really are a together bunch – they've talked a lot amongst themselves about being a band of brothers, a spirit that unites them all – not just the starters, but the walk-ons and managers... they kinda have a collective strength that they wouldn't have as individuals."*

We all need an outlet. Through impermeable relationships, the outlet is "togetherness." Company team members having each other's backs and working together with a mission mindset and toward the same vision through the values they share.

During the 2018 Final Four championship, the statement below was written in Marc Tracy's New York Times piece, "Why Catholic Colleges Excel at Basketball."[160]

> *Villanova's President, the Rev. Peter M. Donohue, hosts an opening Mass for athletes every year, where he reminds them, they are ambassadors for the university's mission. "To have our charisma move on," he said, using a dogma-tinged Greek word for spirit, "the banner needs to be carried." Banners aren't typically carried by one person, but by the team, the group, and the organization.*
>
> *In the mid-1900s, the Catholic Church's attraction to basketball could essentially be distilled to one primary motive: it was a cheap sport. Local priests and nuns realized that basketball,*

> *with its team-focused nature, was an ideal way to engage inner-city youth. The Church's approach was inclusive, welcoming everyone irrespective of ethnicity, socio-economic standing, or gender. Basketball was a game for all. As the years passed, these roots deepened. The youth who started in Catholic schools often transitioned to Catholic colleges and universities, continuing their basketball journey.*
>
> *For St. Joseph's Coach Phil Martelli, these teachings comport with the sport that he called the "greatest societal experiment."*
>
> *"In basketball, it doesn't matter if you're black or white, rich or poor, city or suburbs," said Martelli.... "And in the Catholic faith, you shouldn't be measured by those things — your W-2 or what you drive. You should be measured by your character."*

This societal experiment created relationships and bonds derived from an open-minded culture that encouraged all to be participants. The power of these connections became particularly evident at the collegiate level when, in 2018, of the sixty-four teams in the tournament, eight hailed from Catholic schools, with two advancing to the prestigious Final Four.

Collaboration

Collaboration – the action created by working jointly with someone to produce or create something.[161]

It's beautifully expressed—something *"working jointly with someone."* From Disney in the 1930s to modern giants like Google, workspaces have always buzzed with collaboration—sparking ideas over a latte or casual hallway encounters. These interactions, or as Noyce would call them, 'gatherings,' yield wonderful outcomes. Beauty is not just reflected in the atmosphere around us but also, more importantly, manifests in the dialogue we have with the people around us— learning, gathering, creating together—collaborating.[162]

When Open-Ended Logic weaves through organizations and teams, collaboration emerges as a united endeavor. In this space, individuals set aside external differences, uniting to shape missions that align with the vision. Collaborative gatherings serve as venues for crafting this mission and vision. They are environments where ideas can freely flow, be evaluated, and even dismissed without resentment or contempt.

In these spaces, CEOs set aside their titles, signaling that egos have no place within the collaboration room. This levels the playing field, fostering an environment where ideas, innovation, and outcomes can thrive. Collaboration serves as the connecting link between individuals, silos, teams, departments, and even nations. It is the adhesive that forms and strengthens impermeable relationships.

"Buttfaces" Rule

Phil Knight, co-founder and chairman emeritus of Nike, dedicated an immense amount of effort and determination throughout his career in the shoe business. The roller-coaster journey Knight undertook to elevate Nike to its towering status today genuinely constitutes one of the great success stories of our era. Delving into Phil Knight's memoir, *Shoe*

Dog, felt akin to immersing oneself in J.D. Salinger's *The Catcher in the Rye* and Simon Sinek's *Start with Why*, with a sprinkle of John Grisham's narrative intrigue. Knight laid everything bare in his account.

Knight's team was composed of many intelligent individuals, and he mentions that, initially, a majority had an accounting background. These dedicated individuals, whom Knight affectionately referred to as his "Buttfaces" in the late '70s, deeply cared for, respected, and were committed to one another. They were Knight's trusted misfits.

Nike's financial situation constantly teetered due to its explosive growth. Knight faced a dilemma: either take the company public or risk bankruptcy because of the relentless expansion year after year. He believed in the philosophy, "you grow or die," and he had no intention of choosing the latter. This ambitious approach led to significant challenges, such as banks slashing Nike's credit, government lawsuits instigated by envious competitors, and the relentless issue of consistently outselling their supply—they simply couldn't meet the surging demand.

Outselling may appear as a minor concern, but the real challenges of growth arise when a company can't produce products quickly enough to meet demand. Like Noyce's gatherings in the hallways, Knight's gatherings took place in a hotel, away from headquarters. Here, he and his team would lay everything out and brainstorm the necessary steps to safeguard the company and foster continued growth.

"Buttfaces" became the term of choice during Knight's team gatherings, and he included himself in the mix, expecting to be treated just like any other member. Discussions in these meetings were geared towards the company's betterment. Every idea was open for commentary, free from contempt or fear of repercussions. Ego had no place in Knight's demeanor. When there was an opportunity for a team member to sell or contribute to the business, Knight would send them off, often not expecting to touch base for months. He anticipated their success, not merely hoping for it. His unique trust in his team not only reduced Nike's costs but also bolstered its growth potential.

Knight embraces the leadership motto of General Patton: "Don't tell people how to do things, tell them what to do and let them surprise you with the results." He applied this with Jeff Johnson, Nike's first official team member, and found it so effective that he continued using this approach. "Even though we knew we might fail—and the odds were that we'd probably not succeed—none of the early Nike group doubted our eventual success," Knight once shared with Maxim. "We reinforced each other's beliefs—a quintessential David vs. Goliath mindset." Such is the strength of a team built on trusting relationships.[163,164]

Collision and Chance Encounters

Remote work became a new way to conduct business in the '90s and 2000s and then exploded once Covid went rampant in 2020. It not only was the safe alternative, but offered cost savings for companies and provided flexibility to team members. For instance, IBM saved over $100 million annually by allowing remote work— and this was before the pandemic. Such flexibility signifies open-mindedness, enabling team members to work from virtually anywhere. However, the importance of face-to-face interactions and nurturing close-knit relationships shifted some of this perspective. Recognizing the value of physical proximity in team building, Meta once offered $10,000 bonuses to encourage team members to live near the office, aiming to increase collaborative work hours. This belief is coming back stronger than ever as we've witnessed the downward spiral for our teams and organizations lacking and experiencing togetherness.[165]

What Noyce called gatherings Samsung VP, Scot Birnbaum, speaks of a collision of team members. Harvard Business Review went on to state, "Chance encounters and interactions between knowledge workers improve performance." How can knowledge transfer if dialogue is diminishing?

We've discovered that face-to-face interactions are paramount. Birnbaum's idea of prompting team members to "collide" holds merit. Data suggests that creating collisions—chance encounters and unplanned interactions between knowledge workers, both inside and outside the organization—boosts performance.[166]

Is every organization going to operate at their maximum revenue per team member? Not exactly. Yet, the opportunity businesses have in front of them is to build with pieces that create better-to-best encounters and good to insanely great organizations.

Cadbury and Hershey, both known for great chocolate, built actual cities for their team members for safety reasons. However, the benefits didn't stop there. These leaders knew the importance of a strong, healthy, team member-driven organization and showed kindness through action every day. They were building impermeable relationships with each team member by ensuring quality of life.

Impermeable relationships produce unlimited dividends. Do Google's teams recognize they are swayed to not leave the complex when they take advantage of free lunches? This is an investment that Google is willing to embrace in order to say, "You're welcome to leave, yet we'll feed you if you stay and visit." This is another piece that promotes community with the organization by encouraging people to bond over lunch and build bridges between different departments. Community along with consistent collaboration creates impermeable relationships. If the devils in the details, a bit of heaven is on the other side of taking the little details seriously.

Well-Known Impermeable Relationships

- Richard Cadbury & George Cadbury (Cadbury)
- Warren Buffet & Charlie Munger (Berkshire Hathaway)
- Joanna & Chip Gaines (Magnolia Network)
- Walt & Roy Disney (Disney)
- Billy Graham & Walter Herbert Smyth (Billy Graham Ministries)
- Bill Gates & Paul Allen (Microsoft)
- Josephine Esther Mentzer & Joseph Lauter (Estée Lauder)
- Claude Monet, Paul Durand-Ruel, & Gustave Caillebotte (Artist, art dealer, benefactor)
- Dr. Dre & Jimmy Iovine (Beats)
- Serge Brin & Larry Page (Google)
- Bill Hewlett & Dave Packard (Hewlett-Packard)
- David Green & Barbara Green (Hobby Lobby)
- Ben Cohen & Jerry Greenfield (Ben & Jerry's Ice Cream)
- Pierre Omidyar & Jeffrey Skoll (eBay)
- William Proctor & James Gamble (Procter & Gamble)
- Wilbur & Orville Wright (First manned aircraft)
- John Lasseter & Edwin Catmull (Pixar/Disney Animation Studios)
- Phil Knight & his team of Buttfaces (Nike)
- Vanessa Yakobson & Ari Yakobson (Blo Blow Dry Bar)
- Steve Jobs & Steve Wozniak (Apple)
- Kevin Systrom & Mike Krieger (Instagram)
- Tom Murphy & Dan Burke (Capital Cities Broadcasting)

Tom Murphy and Dan Burke were probably the greatest two-person combination in management that the world has ever seen or maybe ever will see.

Warren Buffett

Frontline First

Many of the most successful websites and apps stem from seeking feedback from end users. Yet, some companies perilously assume that users might not truly know what they desire, banking on the hope that whatever they produce will gain traction. While hope can be an inherent feeling when introducing a new product, it shouldn't be mistaken for a business plan or strategy, especially when pursuing longevity.

The "frontline" comprises individuals who interact most directly and frequently with customers. In today's digital age of texting, emailing, and occasional phone calls, it's the frontline team members who engage most deeply with end users -- the consumer. They provide a firsthand experience of the organization, reflecting product functionality, service quality, and the overall customer experience. While training is crucial, it's even more important for this excellence to be inherent in every frontline team member. Acknowledging their significance both verbally and through actions of appreciation and gratitude is vital.

The best question any organization should be asking themselves is, "What if our frontline thought like a CEO but most importantly, thought like a consumer?"

Environment of Respect

Gone are the days when respect was something to be earned. Now, respect is a gift, freely extended to all from the outset, or should be. Though it's a simple gesture, its impact is profound and lasting, yet, just as quickly as it's given, it can be retracted.

Respect is not another word for trust. While respecting you signifies acknowledging and valuing your worth as an individual, it doesn't automatically mean I trust you. Trust is something that's built over time. Viewing respect as an immediate, mutual exchange provides a foundation from the moment we meet. Respect is the first step; trust is the journey.

Respect for people, what they do, and their importance to the vision is where relationship-building begins. It's essential not just to know what someone does, but to genuinely understand who they are and how they integrate into the organization's larger tapestry. Every person, and their role, is a unique thread in the intricate fabric of the organization's ecosystem.

Walt ensured that his Imagineers truly understood the Disneyland experience from the guest's perspective. By immersing them in the environment - waiting in lines, riding the attractions, and interacting with both the attractions and the Cast Members - he wanted them to gain insights directly from the ground. Listening to the spontaneous feedback of guests and observing their interactions gave these creators invaluable insights. This hands-on approach, a tradition embodied still today, ensures that Disneyland continually evolves, refining its magic and always striving to exceed guest expectations and making people happy.[167]

Starbucks prioritizes equipping its frontline staff with the necessary tools to handle challenging customer interactions. Through a comprehensive two-week training focused on managing difficult customers, Starbucks empowers its team members to navigate crucial conversations effectively. Intentionally managing customer relationships is an opportunity for every team member to be a part of the successful customer service process, turning what could be discouraging outcomes into positive experiences.

Known for their ultra-friendly and righteous love for the customer, Zappos creates an environment of respect and care over the phone. They do this because a respectful culture is at the core of the business, as it began with its late founder, Tony Hsieh. While most companies are monitoring phone calls in customer service call centers around the globe and insisting on shorter conversations, Zappos looks at talk time a little differently. Their belief is that service is of the utmost importance, and they're willing to put their money where their mouths are by insisting that the customer service agent, or "Customer Loyalty Team Member," as they're called at Zappos, gives the customer their best and develops a relationship with not only that agent, but Zappos as a whole.

The onus is on that representative to offer a solution instead of a cookie-cutter policy or procedure. The representative has total autonomy to execute greatness with every call, and they continuously deliver unparalleled services. Tony Hsieh explained in his book, Delivering Happiness, that:

> *"I think the main thing is just trust [the customer service reps] and let them make their own decisions. Most call centers are set up by policies and so the actual person that's answering the phone doesn't really have the ability to do anything. If you call most customer service places, and you ask for anything that's not normal they have to talk to a supervisor or just say 'oh our policy doesn't allow that' and whatever.*
>
> *So, we generally try to stay away from policies, we just ask our reps to do whatever they feel is the right thing to do for the customer and the company. And that's actually really uncomfortable for a lot of reps that come from other call centers. We kind of have to untrain their bad habits. But I think [the customer service reps] are generally not happy because they don't have control over the situation whereas Zappos... there's really nothing that a rep can't do so there's no reason to ever escalate."*[168]

This innovative approach means Zappos doesn't have to lean heavily on discounts or promotions to generate 75 percent of its revenues. Instead, these revenues are driven by repeat customers. Even more noteworthy is the fact that 44 percent of their new clientele comes from referrals, which stands as testament to the potency of word-of-mouth marketing. They've positioned Zappos in the mind of the customer for a predictable outcome of WOWness.

The 80-to-8 Rule

When we think we've mastered "WOW," we're most vulnerable. "80 to 8" isn't necessarily a rule; rather, it's a stat that shows just how much we don't know. An enlightening fact is that 80 percent of CEOs today believe they have exceptional customer service. This is a cloud most execs should step off, because only 8 percent of these companies' customers agree.

It's worth repeating:

80 percent of CEOs today believe they have exceptional customer service, but only 8 percent of those CEOs' customers think the same. [169,170]

When companies start banking on the fact that neglecting the frontline is okay, customers will quickly remind them that's not a profitable idea. Customers are defecting to more and more customer centric organizations that have their finger on the pulse of their frontline instead of only worrying about their shareholders.

With all of this "WOWness", how does Zappos make money? They know that by consistently wowing the consumer through the frontline, they will see results in acquiring and maintaining long term, profitable customers.

The focus? Frontline and Customer First

Employee Experience = Customer Experience

EX = CX

Tracy Maylett, E.D.
The Employee Experience:
How to Attract Talent, Retain Top Performers, and Drive Results[171]

Building the Team around Impermeable Relationships

Building teams begins with individuals who are aligned on the vision, mission, and values (VMV). If an individual, group, or organization is not focused and driven by the VMV, the foundational framework supporting impermeable relationships falters, at best.

"Expedition behavior" is a term derived from the '60s, when famed outdoorsman Paul Petzoldt created the National Outdoor Leadership School. Through Petzoldt's adventures dating back to 1920, he realized that several interesting behaviors surfaced quickly in groups he worked with. The term "expedition behavior" gained traction and now illustrates the natural way team's bond. When a group ventures out into the wilderness for days on end, facades vanish quickly, exposing genuine attitudes of people now confronted with hunger, fatigue, and disorientation, all while their work ethic and overall positive or negative responses come to the fore.

What Petzoldt realized is that it didn't matter what environment one was in—whether in business, education, or the wilderness, the key is to have positive expedition behavior to succeed as an individual or group.

Petzoldt identified keys to good expedition behavior:

- Serve the mission and the goals of the group.
- Be as concerned for others as you are for yourself.
- Treat everyone with dignity and respect.
- Support leadership and growth in everyone.
- Respect the cultures you contact.
- Be kind and open-hearted.
- Do your share and stay organized.
- Help others, but don't routinely do their work.
- Model integrity by being honest and accountable.
- Admit and correct your mistakes.[172]

Expeditions in the wilderness unify teams by forming, reinforcing, and mending solid relationships or as Paradigm Shift's CVO, Jerrod Murr, coined it, "Shared Experiences." Although Shared Experiences could be anything from a lunch to a retreat, Petzoldt noted them as naturally fostering ties as the team must rely on each member to fulfill their role and back everyone simultaneously. Through these steady, small efforts and a positive mindset, they discover that more can be achieved collectively.

With positive expedition behavior, the more you contribute to the team's goal, the more achievable the mission becomes for both you and the team. For expedition behavior to genuinely take root, there needs to be clarity and comprehension, with every team member able to articulate the goal and mission. If the team can't articulate the goal, it's on a trajectory toward an unclear mission, leading to diminished trust and resulting in little to no accountability.

Culture of Trust & Safety

Make Moments Matter

Wayne and Diane Tesch

Certainly, our behaviors, decisions, and thought processes vary based on our perception of safety versus danger. When posed with the question of operating differently in safe versus unsafe zones, many might immediately envision contrasting environments: the familiarity and comfort of one's home versus the uncertainties of a shelter in a foreign country. This question underscores the breadth of human adaptability and how our mindsets shift in response to different circumstances. It also speaks to our innate instincts for survival and protection, which can activate differently depending on our environment. The comparison emphasizes the adaptability of human behavior and thought in diverse situations.

In *The Culture Code*, Daniel Coyle demonstrates that culture is shaped by the degree of safety in an environment, influencing the distinction between strong and weak teams. Safety is emphasized as the default state of affairs. Such is its significance that one of the NBA's most triumphant coaches, Greg Popovich, has dedicated over 30 years cultivating it.[173]

Popovich begins by working with his organization to identify the right individuals even before the San Antonio Spurs officially bring a player onboard. He assesses each player's character and determines how seamlessly that person will integrate with the team—an essential process that Popovich himself oversees to establish a foundation of trust. Before signing Tim Duncan, he traveled to the Bahamas and spent four days understanding Duncan and gauging how he would mesh with the team. It's not common for a coach to dine with and meet the family and friends of a player to gain a deeper insight into the player's character. This is Popovich's way of ensuring a predictable result while forging an impermeable relationship.

It's not only his high-profile players; Popovich connects with everyone. He knows his team, and in turn, his team knows him. When he raises his voice at his star players, they understand they are still in a safe space due to the foundation and elements that have been put in place to construct the player-coach relationship up to that moment.

When people connect through genuine organic situations, these circumstances foster trust and mutual support. Safety doesn't imply that players or team members will never depart due to natural attrition or other factors. The aim is to extract the utmost potential from both the individual and the collective team. Nearly all significant contributions to our environment and society began with one person and progressed through a team that ultimately delivered the end result. Building trust originates from being trustworthy. Start at the center - you.

Strong Results through Engagement

People are pivotal to achieving the outcomes we desire. Everyone will encounter confrontation with someone who doesn't align with the vision, mission, and values of the team. Such confrontations are inevitable. Individuals also evolve due to circumstances unrelated to any internal dynamics within the organization. We cannot expect everyone to be content 100 percent of the time. That is an unrealistic expectation.

Rebecca Ray, PhD, when interviewed by Fast Company's Mark Crowley, stated about Quicken Loans that "few companies have committed themselves to creating a positive and enabling workplace, which they fully leverage to drive high performance."[174]

Quicken Loans (Rocket Companies) founder and chairman Daniel Gilbert annually engages with team members by first updating the company's key values and then training all new team members in an eight-hour session. This intense commitment to engagement has won the hearts of team members and has, in effect, made Quicken Loans a billion-dollar company with a team member base of 17,000 in 2021.[175]

Passing the baton, the new CEO as of 2017, Jay Farner, holds engagement meetings with team members where a "no topic is off limits" discussion ensues. Out of the suggestions presented, 900 were implemented in a single year. Quicken Loans, headquartered in Detroit, Michigan, ranked fourteenth on the best places to work in 2017 and has secured a spot on that list for fifteen years.

This is straight from the Quicken Loans website under "Always raising our level of awareness":

> *As Yogi Berra said, "You can see a lot just by looking. Keep your head up."*
>
> *Look. Be curious. Notice what is actually happening around you.*
>
> *Really notice. Listen. Listen to your clients. In fact, listen to everyone. Everything starts with awareness. Being alert. Being awake. Tuning in to the frequency.*
>
> *It's a perpetual choice to both stay aware and raise your level of awareness.*
>
> *Our future, growth, innovation, and success start with the thousands of eyeballs of our team members. That's you.*[176]

Engagement is a crucial component that can yield exceptional success or, in its absence, produce subpar results. It's a fact, especially in an environment where work is increasing and companies are hiring fast, that people want to feel cared for and respected, and to enjoy their workplace. Why are nice people winning? Team members will work harder and smarter and work for the VMV more than ever if they enjoy the company where they are spending most of their time during the week.

Here are just a few dividends that highly engaged organizations recognize from intentionally devoting time, training, and attention to engagement.

- 41 percent reduction in absenteeism
- 21 percent increase in profitability
- 17 percent increase in productivity
- 10 percent increase in customer ratings
- 20 percent increase in sales
- 59 percent lower turnover
- 58 percent fewer patient safety incidents
- 70 percent fewer team member safety incidents
- 28 percent less shrinkage
- 40 percent fewer quality incidents/defects[177,178,179]

CEOs are realizing that financial performance is intricately linked to the work environment in which team members immerse themselves daily. Environment isn't so much about the physical location where a team member works, but more about the atmosphere, engagement, and interaction among the workforce. Engagement trumps all else.

William Kahn, professor of organizational behavior at Boston University's Questrom School of Business, is credited as the founding father of the term *"engagement,"* which originated in the 1990s. Organizational members seemed to unconsciously pose themselves three questions in each situation and personally engage or disengage depending on the answers. The questions were:

1. How meaningful is it for me to bring myself into this performance?
2. How safe is it to do so?
3. How available am I to do so?[180]

He later tweeted, *"Engagement is about being your best self, not productivity."*

The three components Kahn taught are:

1. **Psychological meaningfulness:** a sense that their work was worthwhile and made a difference.
2. **Psychological safety:** a feeling they were valued, accepted, and respected—and able to perform in a positive work.
3. **Availability:** routinely feeling secure and self-confident while possessing the emotional and psychological energies to perform their job.

Kahn's discoveries remain relevant today and should provide solace to Human Relations departments in search of the next element that motivates and kindles excellence within organizations. This also indicates that solutions aren't solely about allocating more funds and incentives; instead, we face the foundational element known as time. As Dan Sullivan and Dr. Benjamin Hardy states in *Who Not How*, time is time, attention is the crown jewel. Time, fundamentally, is the cornerstone of good parenting and now, good leadership.[181,182,183]

Time encompasses engagement by executives, such as Noyce's gatherings, Walt's drop-ins to the animation department, and Southwest Airlines founder and then-CEO Herb Kelleher's custom of donning costumes and mingling with mechanics in an aircraft hangar at midnight. It's this caliber of engagement that produces monumental, impactful results and spreads virally throughout the organization. Such moments of engagement and genuine transparency filter out the transient participants, inspire individuals to reach their utmost potential, and acknowledge the worth in uplifting those around them.

Thank You Structure + Thank You Culture =

Long-term Productive Frontline & Profitable Customers

Vibe

I don't trust words, I trust vibes... people can tell you anything, but vibe tells you everything.

Anonymous

Vibe: a person's emotional state or the atmosphere of a place as communicated to and felt by others.[184]

What vibe are you giving the world? Some might say, "I don't get good juju from that place" or "what an awesome vibe!" Apple, Target, Starbucks, Ritz-Carlton, Walmart, Hertz, Southwest, the corner convenience store or the local casino all give us a window into the vibes we are exposed to every day. While culture is the internal experience of the organization, the vibe is the external experience—the fragrance being injected into the atmosphere that surrounds the consumer's experience every second.

These brands represent specific vibes that are so distinct we can dissect down to a phrase, a scent, or even just a word how they feel to us as well as the very reasons we love or choose to ignore them. We gravitate to vibe more than any other mechanism because vibe plays into our emotional state.

Your company's vibe can create a long-term advocate or a short-term Reddit critic.

In your mind, consider the brands mentioned and pinpoint one word that encapsulates the vibe of each. Why does the vibe hold such significance in today's environment? The definition provides the answer: our emotional state... "felt by others." For everyone, including individuals, teams, and organizations, Maya Angelou's statement rings profoundly true: "People will forget what you said, people will forget what you did, but people will never forget how you made them feel." The emotional value of the vibe is paramount to the experience we desire as consumers. We are aware of predictable outcomes and remember how we feel when we enter an establishment, regardless of whether it's the corner convenience store or the Ritz Carlton.

There's a rationale behind every decision, and casinos understand the power of setting the right vibe. The music, strategically placed tables, the bar, the eateries, slot machines arranged to showcase dazzling lights, and the noises signaling the next dopamine boost all play a role. Yet, casinos that solely rely on vibrant lights and music fall short unless the individuals within the organization emit the correct vibe: We're here to cater to you and enhance the emotional experience of a positive vibe.

Bernadette Jiwa states that "experience is the new form of currency." From this claim, we can deduce that experience encompasses both how we feel and what we undertake. While many might consider the latter as the primary focus, it's crucial to acknowledge the influence of feelings on our experiences. Given this perspective, the vibe emerges as the principal output of our organization, and the service and products we provide become secondary outputs. Samuel Truett Cathy, founder of Chick-fil-A, recognized that they were in the service business and happened to sell chicken.

More than ever before, the consumer prefers experiences over tangibles—it's how a consumer feels that draws them down a pathway. If this is true, would it be safe to say that the emotional vibe we display is in fact one of our most important ways to differentiate? This may be why social marketing is towering over the conventional marketing space. Sure, we've experienced "feelings" toward products or organizations since the turn of the century through media, primarily through radio and television. Yet, social media places us so much closer to the people using these products and services. "I want to feel like that" is really saying, "I want to experience that vibe."

Now, to play devil's advocate, let's argue that social media companies are undergoing both descents and ascents due to the vibes they're emitting, which signal greed and dissatisfaction. We're recognizing that social media and the massive organizations behind each platform are becoming less our advocates and more of an abusive relationship in our lives as we begin to pull back the layers of unethical practices directed at end users. The vibe they exude will inevitably corner them into making choices that may not directly boost profits but are imperative to restore customer trust.

Vibe is asking ourselves; how do we want our customers to feel when they see us, interact with us, and ultimately do business with us? Nailing down these three criteria will help us gauge where our demeanor should be when interacting with anyone outside our organization. Is our vibe different when someone becomes a customer? Not at all. People are relying on the fact that the vibe they initially felt the first time is predictable and will experience it here on out. Consider Dutch Bros., the phenom coffee company exploding out of Oregon.

Dutch Bros. started as a pushcart espresso bar in 1992, by the railroad tracks in downtown Grants Pass, Oregon. In 2022, it was a 600-plus coffee outlet operation, and you can expect a West Coast vibe at each location. The team vibe is that they appreciate your business, and they'll build your drink to please - guaranteed.

As stated on their landing page:

> *"We may sell coffee, but we're in the relationship business. Whether we're slinging drinks or serving up smiles, Dutch Bros is all about you!"*[185]

Dutch Bros. can influence the emotional state of their customers by establishing the right vibe. They can do so because they're clear on the predictable outcome they want their guests to experience. They understand that vibe is emotional in essence. Can we fully govern the emotional state of our clientele? We possess the capacity to draw individuals into our vibe, and Dutch Bros. exemplifies this skillfully. They've transformed a brief drive-thru encounter into a good vibe—cool people who are keen for me to savor the best drink of my life. At least that's the vibe I get.

Values x Behavior = Culture

Demeanor x Experience = Vibe

Demeanor – facial appearance; attitude; poise; presence.[186]

Our demeanor is intrinsically linked to our attitude and composure, which in turn help shape the comprehensive vibe within our teams. Making the vibe an inherent trait of the organization— "We want to convey this"—allows us to set the predictable outcome. This is what organizations such as Dutch Bros. and Raising Cane's have executed so well, setting a standard for the desired vibe so that all frontline staff can embrace and replicate it. In many other firms, a new hire might be left to their own devices, to either sink or swim. However, within these two businesses, the vibe is central to their training and the expectations that outline "how we, as a company, want to be perceived." This task becomes more straightforward than ever when there's a clear focus on the desired vibe.

Vibe is the external aroma of an organization, and when focus is given to this particular trait, it can positively influence every interaction both within and outside its boundaries. Understand what vibe signifies for your organization, recognize the fragrance you wish to infuse into your environment, and then embrace and project that vibe—it truly matters!

Owning A Phrase of Gratitude

No company has harnessed the power of two simple words of gratitude and transformed them into a signature slogan quite like Chick-fil-A. They've masterfully adopted the phrase "my pleasure" as a standardized expression of gratitude, showcasing their appreciation to patrons at every single one of their over two-thousand locations.

Table the quality of the chicken and the exceptionally brilliant marketing of the cow mastering the art of misspellings, always asking us to "EAT MOR CHIKIN". Beyond those evident triumphs, a guest can step into the Chick-fil-A at 26861 Aliso Creek Road in Aliso Viejo, California, and receive an identical experience to the Chick-fil-A at 1180 6th Ave, New York, New York—a heartfelt greeting followed by the trademark "my pleasure." Instituting consistent models of customer service and cordiality from one coast to the other is among the chief pillars underpinning the brand's success.

How does Chick-fil-A achieve such standardized service excellence? Through rigorous training of their team members. Where else can one observe four distinct generations—Gen-Z, Millennials, Gen-X, and Boomers—collaborating side by side, effortlessly serving up chicken sandwiches, consistently adorned with smiles and always eager to assist guests? This level of service is what you encounter at Chick-fil-A, irrespective of your location or identity.

Samuel Truett Cathy founded the first Chick-fil-A in 1946 in the Atlanta suburb of Hapeville, Georgia. On a visit to a Ritz-Carlton, Cathy said "thank you" to the man behind the counter and was greeted with the response, "my pleasure." From this experience, Cathy's ambition was to adopt this five-star establishment slogan and deliver that same level of energy and appreciation to the customer buying his chicken sandwiches. The slogan creates an experience instead of a transaction, a key factor in the ever-increasing brand loyalty.

At that moment, Cathy thought that customers must feel they're at a luxury establishment.[187]

Associating the brand with these two words, uttered millions of times daily, serves as an additional marketing strategy—a hallmark of courtesy and kindness. It's effective, and because it resonates so deeply with their guests, they are assured of a uniformly positive experience at every Chick-fil-A outlet, owing to the meticulously executed, top-notch service. Why risk going elsewhere with uncertain odds of receiving good service? By centering their foundation on team member training, emphasizing professional growth and customer attentiveness, Chick-fil-A stands at the forefront of companies committed to delivering exceptional service as a daily necessity. The question arises, what can we be saying or doing to show 5-star service, positioning our brand in the minds of guests millions of times each day?

Realizing the purpose behind the phrase and ensuring its consistency relies on a profound understanding of "why" it's essential to address customers in that specific manner. "My pleasure" indeed evokes the sensation of being at an upscale eatery, exactly as Cathy envisioned. The genius in marketing isn't just the cows; it's the intentional emphasis on those two words of gratitude. The cows depicted in advertisements conjure memories of the excellent experience we anticipate every time we consider breakfast, lunch, or dinner at Chick-fil-A, not merely the chicken itself.

Humility and Authentic Gratitude Creates Sustainable Growth and Long-Term Value

At Chick-fil-A, the concept of service modeling is deeply ingrained. Each team member is trained to greet customers with a "Hi, how can I serve you?" and to replace "You're welcome" with "My pleasure!" This is a core component of their training. Teammates undergo a week of watching corporate videos centered around customer interactions more than on food preparation. This aligns with Tony Hsieh's philosophy. His sentiment mirrored Cathy's, though oriented towards footwear: "Zappos is a service company, and we just happen to sell shoes." It's noteworthy that two highly successful companies from completely different sectors share a similar emphasis on the customer's experience with their frontline staff.

Are their prices better than everyone else's? No. In fact, while Chick-fil-A offers a reasonably priced meal, they are costlier than many of their competitors. They don't feature a Value Menu, but, akin to Zappos, they don't need to be the most competitive. Their strategy revolves around consistent, excellent service, delivered day in and day out, ensuring the customer always anticipates a positive, predictable outcome.

This prompts the question: if this premium service philosophy can be integrated into the sale of chicken and shoes, why isn't it incorporated into everything we sell? Is integration the primary? What can we seamlessly incorporate into our ongoing cycle of customer interactions to elevate our service and firmly position our brand in the consumer's mind? It could be the difference between telling a customer "there are drinks in the fridge" to asking a guest, "what drink would you like, we have Evian or Coke-Cola?"

The Power of The Word

- Words can settle disputes
- Words can pollute
- Words can shape the situation
- Words can create a positive future
- Words can create a negative future
- Words can make a poor environment a great one
- Words can make a great environment a poor one
- Words can build impermeable relationships
- Words can destroy impermeable relationships
- Words can make a person feel like they can take on the world
- Words can make a person feel inadequate and forgotten
- Words can motivate a person in your organization to accomplish a huge task
- Words can make a person in your organization underperform
- Words will make the difference

Words can either be toxic or nourishing—choose wisely. Optimize the use of your words as a group, team, or organization, and reap benefits rather than suffer setbacks.

<u>Which would you rather be called?</u>

Student: a person who is studying at a school or college.

Scholar: a distinguished academic.

California School Teacher, Brianna Leonard, welcomes each of her students everyday with the following greeting:

"Hello my young scholar!"

<u>Which would you rather be called?</u>

Customer: a person or organization that buys goods or services from a store or business.

Guest: a person who is invited to visit the home of or take part in a function organized by another.

Which would you rather be called?

Account: An account established by a company to record a customers' transactions related to service under one or more rate schedules.

Partner Client: A client with whom a business maintains a close, long-term, and strategic relationship, often characterized by mutual trust, collaboration, shared goals, and a commitment to joint growth.

Leadership and Development company, Paradigm Shift, calls each customer a "Partner Client":

"We look at every customer as a Partner Client as our goal is to develop leaders and teams for the long-game, which truly requires a partnership."

Which would you rather be called?

Employee: person employed for wages or salary, especially at nonexecutive level.

Team Member / Teammate: a member of a team, especially in a workplace.

The Power of Appreciation From The Top Down

THANKS - A really neglected form of compensation.

Robert Townsend (Avis CEO)

Raising Cane's, another billion-dollar chicken restaurant enterprise, is setting new standards both internally and externally. At Raising Cane's, irrespective of whether you're in marketing, accounting, or even the CEO, as is the case with founder Todd Graves, there's a mandate for everyone to work a minimum of one week annually at one of their now over six-hundred locations. The Greater Baton Rouge Business Report doesn't just label Graves as "CEO," but also adds "fry cook and cashier" to his title. This reflects a deep respect for every role vital for the successful operation of a restaurant. Graves further articulates, "I've done every job, because when we first opened, we didn't have much money... Our culture is deeply rooted in appreciation."

His perspective demonstrates genuine gratitude not just for the customers, but also for the team members of Raising Cane's. The culture has been built from the top down and is deeply rooted in every position in Raising Cane's. Appreciation has a ripple effect - it's contagious and effective. Thousands of team members across various roles within the company sell chicken, and they do so with a smile.

The power of appreciation cannot be understated. Both Walt Disney and Bob Noyce might not have been known for overt praises, but they had their unique ways of expressing gratitude. Disney often voiced appreciation for his team in their absence, and Noyce strengthened those around him with encouragement. In one instance, upon encountering a young engineer in the hallway, the engineer remarked to Noyce, "I bet you stayed up most of the night worrying about me working on that project." Noyce's response — "No, I slept like a baby because I know you're the right person for the job." Such encouragement instilled profound confidence in his team, so much so that explicit words of thanks were often unnecessary.

Disney had a penchant for penning thank-you notes and letters, extending encouragement to many. But more importantly, he dedicated time to his team. He was familiar with his people on a personal level and recognized the value they contributed. For many, they would experience these interactions, quite literally, at the drawing tables.

We're all unique in our ways of showing appreciation. It's vital to recognize that regardless of whether appreciation is conveyed through spoken words of thanks, written notes, or accolades, team members and then, customers, will inevitably feel cherished. Consequently, team members are likely to achieve improved outcomes both in the short and long run.

Why Have *Thank You* Everywhere?

When you navigate the drive-thru at your neighborhood Starbucks, you'll encounter a singular sign as you exit: "Thank you." Why have a gratitude sign at the departure point? The answer is straightforward—they're expressing gratitude for your choice to spend over $5 on a cup of coffee with them.

No business, group, or team member should ever neglect to thank a guest for their business. Serving customers, or guests, is a privilege, and often individuals, whether in higher echelons or at ground level, lose sight of this foundational aspect of business, leading to customer attrition.

Cultivating a culture of gratitude begins by educating team members on the value of thankfulness. In this era dominated by online and mobile social platforms, we've often distanced ourselves from the basics of expressing gratitude. As leaders, the consistent message should revolve around appreciation at every tier. When team members genuinely perceive and experience this appreciation, customers benefit from remarkable experiences. This is where the culture of gratitude takes root. team members who sense recognition and value in their roles consistently outperform across all job facets.

What does true appreciation drive? A Culture of Value and Communicative Excellence. Start the thank-you's today and be consistent.

- Pick up a phone and call a customer or team member to say, "thank you."
- Write thank-you cards to customers.
- Write thank-you cards to staff.

- Give out thank-you cards and ask teams to write one to a customer each week.
- Pick a customer and write an email: "Wanted to say thanks for..."
- Pick a team member and write an email: "Thank you for..."

Organizations that have successfully embraced and internalized the straightforward phrases "thank you" and "my pleasure" see cumulative benefits in daily interactions. Expressing gratitude doesn't incur any cost, yet its return on investment is invaluable. Authentic appreciation is an essential strategy to tap into sustained profitable growth, regardless of perspective.

Ultimately, expressing gratitude fosters loyalty and consistent excellence among both team members and guests. Implementing a "thank you" policy is necessary. The challenge, however, lies in the "how." Training is imperative. Organizations must engage in relentless training, ensuring the brutal consistency so many of our patron's desire.

Thank you for reading!

Vision Is The Narrator

From expressing gratitude to promoting open-mindedness, to engaging in communal activities, and investing both financially and emotionally in individuals, the team member is intricately intertwined with every facet of our organizations. It's a universal truth that organizations which invest more into their workforce reap larger dividends in return.

When individuals collaborate with a focus on enduring benefits, embracing the foundation, framework, and ethos, a synchronicity occurs, propelling both the people and organizations to higher levels of achievement. Vision becomes tangible, underpinned by the heart (values) and manifested through action (mission). Vision defines our daily endeavors—our purpose. In Open-Ended Logic, the narrator embodies this vision.

If vision is the narrator, what is vision telling us of all the things we need to do as team members within the team, group, or organization?

The common thread linking the most successful individuals and organizations—from Cadbury to Hershey, the Wright brothers, Walt Disney, Robert Noyce, Elon Musk, Jeff Bezos, David Green, Grant Cardone, Gordon Moore, Steve Jobs, Dr. Dre, Mark Zuckerberg, and the next wave of prominent figures and entities—are two attributes: persistence and creativity. They consistently demonstrate determination and ingenuity, choosing to embody grit in their relentless quest for excellence. This tenacity is a key component of their success.

Persistence Is The Connector

Our greatest weakness lies in giving up.
The most certain way to succeed is always to try
just one more time.

Thomas Edison

The term 'persistence' is indifferent to race, background, religion, or physical appearance. It isn't concerned with our mannerisms or the way we express ourselves. Persistence is solely focused on whether we rise and relentlessly chase our vision. We have a responsibility to our team, our organization, ourselves, and the narrator—vision—to embody persistence in everything we do.

So, where does all of the other stuff fit in? Things like integrity, accountability, value systems, work ethic, knowledge, and attention to detail? These elements are the components of persistence. We must demonstrate persistence in each of these aspects. Thus, persistence is the driving force behind every individual's actions.

What is expected of us in our organization? Persistence. But the essential question remains: For whom are we being persistent? Is it merely because our supervisor, and their supervisor, expects it? As team members, our persistence shouldn't be aimed at pleasing just one individual within the organization. Persistence propels us towards our envisioned goals. If vision is the guiding voice, shouldn't we be dedicated to that vision? Shouldn't we value it, cherish it, and work towards it daily, propelling ourselves closer through our tasks and our missions?

It's crucial to recognize that we harness funds as a result of our persistence, not the other way around. Through consistently delivering exceptional work, rewards follow.

By the time Phil Knight and his buttfaces were transitioning Nike from sales out of a car trunk to their new office, another passionate young entrepreneur in the heartland of America was also selling products from his trunk. Though his wares were bulkier than sneakers, David Green, along with his wife Barbara, was laying the groundwork for what would become Hobby Lobby. With a $600 bank loan in 1970 used to manufacture and sell miniature frames, Green laid the foundation for a giant in the arts and crafts domain.

While Green was balancing his day job as a TG&Y Store Manager, he spent his nights alongside Barbara in their garage, assembling frames. In just two years, they inaugurated the first Hobby Lobby store, spanning 300 square feet, in Oklahoma. Starting from these modest roots, Hobby Lobby has since expanded to nearly 1,000 locations across 48 states, employing over 43,000 individuals. It would be misleading to suggest that Green's journey with Hobby Lobby was smooth sailing. With each phase of growth, the company faced gargantuan trials, but Green's approach was always to adapt, stretch, and capitalize on every opportunity.

Growth for Hobby Lobby was accompanied by its share of challenges. Whether it was banks refusing to finance when most needed, electricity getting cut off due to unpaid bills even while customers were shopping, or vendors threatening to withhold supply, Green's resilience and determination remained steadfast. Anchored by his profound faith in God and a move-forward mindset, Green pressed on grit. It wasn't until the mid-80s, after facing numerous obstacles that could have sunk the then-emerging enterprise, that he began to witness the fruits of his persistence.[188]

Hobby Lobby's Mission:

- Honoring the Lord in all we do by operating the company in a manner consistent with Biblical principles.
- Offering our customers exceptional selection and value.
- Serving our team members and their families by establishing a work environment and company policies that build character, strengthen individuals, and nurture families.
- Providing a return on the family's investment, sharing the Lord's blessings with our team members, and investing in our community.

With steady tenacity, Green has maintained Hobby Lobby as a 100 percent privately-owned entity. When questioned about the decision not to go public, Green's response emphasizes his values: "We wouldn't be able to give how we see fit." This isn't about accumulating more possessions but about the impact Hobby Lobby can make globally. Philanthropy is a cornerstone for Green, something he intends to be a part of his enduring legacy. Below are just a few of the numerous causes and establishments Hobby Lobby supports:

- OneHope
- Every Home for Christ
- Oral Roberts University
- Museum of the Bible
- YouVersion

With a strong faith in God and a clear mission, Green remains dedicated even after fifty-three years, showing up daily to his office as Hobby Lobby's CEO. He remains steadfastly committed to the vision: "to promote creative arts while upholding Christian values."

To know who or what we're being persistent for, we have to know the vision, we have to understand each mission, and we have to truly live the values inside and outside the organization's four walls.

It's our responsibility to be enthusiastic about persistence and to recognize our power in controlling our level of persistence. We have full autonomy over how persistent we decide to be, regardless of the path, person, situation, or customer we encounter.

Had Steve Jobs not shown a lethal persistence in his belief that he could create a superior phone, we might still be using the BlackBerry with bubble buttons. Without Walt Disney's persistence, Mickey Mouse and the enchanting world of Disneyland might not exist - "Where Dreams Come True." Similarly, if Noyce hadn't joined and then initiated his 'gatherings' at Fairchild Semiconductors, literally hundreds, if not thousands, of companies would not have emerged.

Without persistence driving our core each day we find ourselves at a standstill—in essence, stagnant. Stagnation is not sitting still but regressing. Passion, while valuable, is not synonymous with persistence. There are countless individuals and teams brimming with passion who falter when faced with the need for genuine persistence. They often hesitate to make the necessary sacrifices when the situation demands it. The failure rate spikes when initiatives aren't pursued with steady determination. These initiatives are often those grand projects unveiled with much enthusiasm from the top echelons, only to crumble when faced with the slightest resistance at the grassroots level. Why does this happen? Often, it's due to a disconnect with the frontline right from the outset and a failure to ask the right open-ended questions. This can result in unforeseen outcomes. Both predictability and success hinge on persistence. We truly flourish when we persist.

Persistence is required at every level
and within every person.

Persistence ought to be a fundamental expectation at every level of an organization, from the chairperson to the frontline staff. Persistence is infectious, radiating through the energy of individuals. Embed persistence within the vision and mission and what was once deemed unattainable suddenly unveils a realm of incredible possibilities.

The People of Open-Ended Logic

Whether an organization spans just two individuals or reaches 102,000, Open-Ended Logic serves as the equilibrium between relevance and irrelevance. This intrinsically boils down to culture. As highlighted earlier, culture acts as a catalyst, influencing from the top down and equally from the bottom up.

So, we've had all this talk of Open-Ended Logic – how organizations and groups have implemented, and what that looks like holistically, down to the smallest of details. But what about the individual? What does this responsibility look like to the people? To you – to me?

The responsibility is fairly simple. The ingredients of our tasks, roles and achievements come from being part of an organization. It's essential to comprehend the vision, mission, and values, and then thread these concepts into the following questions:

- How do I make a difference and contribute?
- How do I drive the best results?
- How do I inspire others to accomplish their best results?
- How do I keep from becoming complacent?
- How do I deliver the best service all the time, even when no one is looking?
- How do I build curiosity?
- How do I become more persistent and what does that look like in my world?
- How do I cultivate my own values system that works inside and outside the walls of my organization?

The myriad of questions we pose are what we, as proprietors, leaders, and collaborative members – the team members of an organization – must constantly explore to effectively champion the Vision, Mission, and Values - the VMV. Not one person will ever comprehend your environment better than you do. The answers unquestionably reside within. It always circles back to VMV.

By operating consistently within the VMV framework and relentlessly aiming to elevate our teams through daily enhancements, holding true to our values, we are fulfilling the mission. When the VMV is not only grasped but deeply ingrained in every member, the organization is poised to unlock its full potential – the vision.

This alignment of core, structure and culture enriches the organization and all its stakeholders, from collaborative members to the consumer – our guest. In the end, all will be better for it in our brutal pursuit of reaching beyond our imagination.

The Beginning...

Epilogue

Open-Ended Logic began as an article I wanted to post on my LinkedIn profile several years ago, but quickly it developed into many more words. It became a way for me to express my thoughts, ideas, and theories on paper. I studied and researched the leaders and businesses that thrived and succeeded even though they were faced with adversity and experienced valleys of failure. These stories resonated with and inspired me as I reflected on my past successes and failures. As the pages increased, so did my hunger for deeper understanding and insight into these real-life characters and organizations and their visions, missions, and values.

I reflected on the demise of my own business in 2009. Before this, in 2003, I had experienced the sale of my first business, an internet company. Soon after the sale, a close friend and I partnered, and found ourselves touring China to find the hot new products for my next venture. Although we experienced success for the first few years, business began to drastically decline toward the end of 2008, and within a year I found myself alone and sitting in my car for hours in front of the office, trying to figure out my next move. I was broke and it was my fault, regardless of the poor market conditions. In the end, I had failed, and it stung.

I thought about my family - an amazing wife and four wonderful children. After shaking the failure of defeat off for the moment, I moved quickly—I just needed to get a paycheck for my mind's sake. Within a short time, I found myself working at UPS, loading trucks from 3 a.m. to 7 a.m., running to my car after clocking out, driving home with an hour in between, showering, and heading to my second job, where leadership was kind enough to place me on the 9 a.m. to 6 p.m. slot selling B2B office supplies over the phone. Yes, I was heading toward the Michael Scott of careers. I had neither the time nor the patience to sit and dwell—I needed to move forward.

These are the parts you don't want anyone knowing, or worse, witnessing firsthand. However, this was the period of my life, at the age of 39, when I pulled myself together and began reading like a machine, absorbing anything to define and encourage perseverance in real life. With help from a gracious God, wife, and family, I moved forward. These are the moments that define us, and they force us to dig deep and realize our grit. They wake us up to what's important in our lives. As with the shift from a BMW to a very dated minivan, life changes and then alters our egos. Before we know it, we find ourselves in the thicket, surrounded by brush, where we start swinging the machete, trying to cut down the weeds of life just to find a road - any road. It was in this experience that a new level of business acumen was rooted—including the significance of vision, mission, and values. I never thought about it in my past, but as I submerged myself into this thought, I found the core's value, realizing that it's the linchpin.

I moved on to another great organization in 2014, leading a team, and then moved up to a National Account position working with top-tier organizations. It was during this time, and over the weekend of July 4th, 2017, after reading the passage, *"the rapport the eight of them shared was dynamic and impermeable"* from Leslie Berlin's book *The Man Behind the Microchip*, that I began to realize I was on to something. As I reread the paragraph on 'Noyce's gatherings' over and over and over while focusing intently on the word 'impermeable,' I knew I wanted Open-Ended Logic to become something more than an article.

My intent is that Open-Ended Logic encourages and gives hope to an individual, a team, or an organization so they aspire to greatness and thrive beyond their wildest expectations by focusing on the vision, the mission, and the values. Those are the driving forces to unleash action and build wonderful things.

Appreciation to...

The friends who encouraged me along the way, showing excitement as I explained passages, who read chapters and paragraphs of Open-Ended Logic and then promised that you would read the printed version when complete. I will surely seek you out if I must. Thank you!

The Southwest agent, Greg in the OKC airport, who sees me about two to three weeks every month and checks my bags and says to me each time... "Thank you for paying my paycheck, Kevin, we really appreciate you and your business." Your entire team at the counter is all so friendly, always helpful, and ultra-fast. Each of you exudes your mission and values 10x – Herb would be very proud.

Janette Maxwell, for trekking through run-on sentences to nowhere and guiding my thoughts and words. I appreciate you sticking with it to the end.

Emma Robbins, who edited and pushed me to dig deeper. Thank you and appreciate your insight, persistence, and brilliance.

Krystine Kercher, thank you for the back and forth editing and dealing with my OCD without fail. You and Dan (below) are incredible and appreciate the dedication and determination to helping me see Open-Ended Logic through.

Darlene Shortridge and Dan Mawhinney with 40 Day Publishing, thank you for bringing your eyes and brainpower to the final version and making it real. Darlene passed unexpectedly on September 24, 2022, during the editing process of Open-Ended Logic. She was an inspiration, an encourager, and a light, and she will be forever missed, but more importantly never forgotten. Dan—you're a rock who I have, in a short time, come to trust and appreciate more and more—thank you.

Yenni and David Vance, friends who "wanted" to read Open-Ended Logic, took the final draft, and brought back more thoughtful insight that I am grateful for. I value you both so much and appreciate you dearly.

Benjamín "Benny" Gagliardi, the person who started off being just one of my son's best friends—however, over time I've learned to appreciate his wisdom, love for Christ, and encouragement. He coined a phrase during one of our visits: "Who are we to think we can bypass the valley?" How profound and encouraging. Thank you and love you.

David Green, thank you for investing in me at a young age and being one of the best mentors an entrepreneur could ever ask for. Although it was a failing experience, you stuck by me and continued to offer mental and spiritual support, prayer, and business advisory among a lot of lunches. You are truly one of the greatest entrepreneurs of this century and having you spend your time with me meant so much. You live and breathe true vision, mission and values every day. I do appreciate you and Barbara more than words could express.

Terry "T" McKever, one of my closest friends, business advisor, attorney, and just one of the kindest souls. You are always there when I need help, you asked questions, and you made me think differently when laying my thoughts out. You show your love through your constant servant leadership style—never asking for anything but always giving. I appreciate you more than words could ever describe, my friend. You're not just a blessing to me but to my entire family—thank you!

Jerrod Murr, for being a consistent voice of inspiration and insight, offering your wisdom with a dash of radicalness. One of the hardest and most dedicated Founders and Chief Visionary Officers who doesn't just talk about values but embodies them every single day.

My second set of parents, Hubert and Glenda Morris. You continue to show true love and support with your kids and grandkids alike— always there in times of need and encouragement. You are a blessing to me and so many others around the world, literally, who you've touched. Thank you for your willingness to listen to my thoughts and for letting me hog the kitchen table for many years when we visited your home as I researched and typed away.

My sister and my brother-in-law, Kelly and Troy Paino (nieces Sophia & Chloe), my brother and sister-in-law, Kyle and Kami Ragsdale (niece Khory & nephew Kayden), and my brother and sister-in-law, Kannin and Candace Ragsdale (nephews Gavin, Declan & Daxton). Although we are all separated to the ends of the continent, I value the foundation we built with each other—it's impermeable. Because of a rich closeness in the past, we have the innate ability to pick up where we left off without thought, and that's pretty cool. I sincerely love you and appreciate your encouragement.

My parents, Hal, and Linda Ragsdale:

Mom, you would have been my first editor for sure. You would have been there supporting me at the end of every chapter and with every thought. I appreciated you listening to my ideas and dreams when I was a kid and younger adult before your passing, and always saying, "Go for it." The final version may have not been the book you would have written (Mom wrote fiction), but through me, your words made it to print because you instilled the incredible values every day of your life through your kindness and generosity in everything you did. I love and still miss you terribly.

Dad, I haven't forgotten the times you took me on many of your sales trips, traveling the back roads of Missouri, Oklahoma, and Kansas, going from town to town, selling garments to the smalltown retailers. I learned the lessons of sales, grit, tenacity, and kindness all while witnessing what a fearless protector you were. We always had food, we were always safe, and we always knew we were loved. You were a great man and especially a great dad. I love and miss you.

Brianna Leonard, our first child and an incredible big sister and daughter to our family who always encouraged me throughout this lengthy 6-7 years of writing. You are a remarkable person and I thank God for you (and all our kiddos) every day.

Bella Ragsdale, for the consistent encouragement, support and brutal honesty :) always! You are a light to this family!

My daughter, Savanna Ragsdale, who read OEL and asked wonderful questions, challenged my thoughts ("dad, why do you insist on definitions?" :) and wording - thank you for taking part of your summer days to read your dad's book. Love you, Princess!

My son and business partner, Adam Ragsdale, who read and reread and then asked, "Hey Dad, what if you tried this or that?" many times over. Your corrections and editing (several drafts) and cover design all made sense and most of it made it to print... and thank you for your consistent encouragement – Love you, Champ!

All my incredible kiddos, Brianna (Breezie), Adam (Champ), Savanna (Savi / Princess), and Isabella (Bella-Boo / LilHam), and to my son-in-law, John (J-dawg), and daughter-in-law, Marin (Mar). You are all the most important beings to your mom's and my world. I wouldn't be who I am without you – I learn from you. You truly make me want to be a better person and we are indeed the BFW—I love you so much and thank you!

My bride, Deanna, who took a 300+ page spiral brick and condensed it to a smaller brick that made more sense for others to understand and edit. You then helped edit twice more on the final draft, appeasing my OCD meticulously with Adam, looking over every word and punctuation. You listened, challenged my thoughts and ideas, ever injecting the right words and phrases to stick with, all during a period where time was difficult to find. You define true servant leadership every day through your work and family. I love and truly thank you.

And last but certainly not least, God. Through all my many failures and meager successes, both personal and in business, thank You for the constant reminder that YOU have given me a hope and a future. I felt Your push and tug to finish what I started with Open-Ended Logic—thank You. Words cannot express my gratitude for Your salvation, forgiveness, and grace. I love You. I thank You and believe in You with all my heart.

About The Author

Kevin Ragsdale is a husband and dad of four pretty amazing kids and extended family. From selling an internet company in 2003, to losing a business in 2009 and juggling two jobs to sustain his family, Kevin's journey from then until now, ultimately, has led to his passion in transforming the vision, mission, and values into the organizational ecosystem. It is in this environment individuals can thrive and lead within their domains, catapulting both their career and the organization's long-term profit.

Visit Kevin on **The Voca App** and request his time for a one-on-one call or learn more by visiting KRagsdale.com or email contact@Kragsdale.com.

Endnotes

1. David McCullough, *The Wright Brothers*

2. https://www.jfklibrary.org/asset-viewer/archives/JFKPOF/040/JFKPOF-040-001

3. Bob Iger, *Ride of a Lifetime*

4. Jim Collins, *Great by Choice*

5. https://web.stanford.edu/dept/SUL/sites/mac/parc.html

6. Leslie Berlin, *The Man Behind the Microchip*

7. *The Adventures of Prince Achmed*, 1926

8. Pat Williams with Jim Denney, *How to be like Walt*

9. https://cronkitehhh.jmc.asu.edu/blog/2015/03/another-one-of-walts-screwy-ideas/

10. https://sites.disney.com/waltdisneyimagineering/our-story/

11. https://sites.disney.com/waltdisneyimagineering/our-story/

12. Pat Williams with Jim Denney, How to be like Walt

13. http://fedexlegends.info/zapmail/zapmail.html

14. Jonathan Coopersmith, "The Failure of Fax: When a Vision Is Not Enough," Business and Economic History 23, no.1 1994: 272-282. https://www.jstor.org/stable/23702852

15. https://www.businessnewsdaily.com/3882-vision-statement.html

16. https://www.forbes.com/sites/johnkoter/2013/10/14/the- reason-most-company-vision-statements-arent-effective/?sh=38366d1f2dc7

17. Google definition

18. Will Dean, *It Takes a Tribe: Building the Tough Mudder Movement*, Sept. 12, 2017

19. https://www.forthechildren.org/about-us/camps

20. For The Children - 2021 FTC Stats-and-Facts.pdf

21. Leslie Berlin, *The Man Behind the Microchip*

22. computerhistory.org

23. Marty Cagen, *INSPIRED*

24. raisingcanes.com

25. https://mays.tamu.edu/maysnews/2010/03/31/when-life- gives-you-lemons/

26. SimonSinek.com

27. sinekpartners.typepad.com

28. http://www.bobpearlman.org/Learning21/Mission- percent20and-percent20Vision.htm

29. http://www.eductionworld.com/a_admin/admin/admin229.shtml Decide on consistent documentation!

30. https://www.thevaluable500.com/member/virgin-atlantic#:~:text=Our%20vision%20at%20Virgin%20Atlantic,and%20where%20they%20can%20thrive.

31. thefreedictionary.com

32. https://www.ashland.k12.mo.us/o/primary/page/primary- school-mission-vision-collaborative-commitments

33. https://thewaltdisneycompany.com/#:~:text=The%20mission %20of%20The%20Walt,the%20world's%20premier%20entert ainment%20company.

34. https://about.google/

35. https://about.google/philosophy/

36. Harvard Business Review Nov-Dec 2017, p. 17

37. https://mission-statement.com/google/

38. https://www.amazon.jobs/en/landing_pages/consumer- admin

39. Chipotle's "About Us" page in 2017 - page not found on website in 2019

40. https://chipotle.com/foodsafety

41. https://mission-statement.com/disney/

42. Adam Grant, *Originals*

43. https://www.bridgewater.com/principles-and-culture

44. https://corporate.virginatlantic.com/gb/en/our-story.html

45. https://businessmodelanalyst.com/trader-joes-business- model/

46. https://www.traderjoes.com/home/about-us

47. https://www.liveabout.com/food-beverage-mission- statements-4068551

48. https://www.zappos.com/about/what-we-live-by#:~:text=Since%20our%20humble%20beginnings%2C%20Z appos,long%2Dterm%2C%20sustainable%20way.

49. https://www.forbes.com/sites/micahsolomon/2016/01/26/what-any-business-can-learn-from-the-way-nordstrom-handles-customer-service/?sh=4cbc12e75b9e

50. https://topworkplaces.com/company/hubspot-inc/boston/

51. https://www.hubspot.com/our-story

52. https://www.redonline.co.uk/wellbeing/

53. Tom Peters, *In Search of Excellence - Point Five of Eight Basic Principles*

54. Google Dictionary

55. Enron – Corporate values – the story of demise

56. Enron's 65-page Code of Ethics can be found at https://www.fbi.gov/history/artifacts/enron-code-of-ethics

57. Seth Godin, *Tribes*

58. PS.company

59. https://www.dunkindonuts.com/en/about/about-us

60. https://mission-statement.com/disney/

61. https://jobs.disneycareers.com/our-culture

62. http://www.idsnews.com/article/1999/04/subway-jared- archive

63. https://www.heraldtimesonline.com/story/news/crime/2021/11/02/jared-fogle-subway-jared-timeline-career-and-downfall/6253368001/

64. https://studylib.net/doc/9010159/officemax-%E2%80%93- business-profile

65. https://www.berkshirehathaway.com/letters/1978.html

66. https://www.berkshirehathaway.com/letters/2013ltr.pdf

67. www.thepostgame.com/blog/throwback/201501/ucla-bruins- 88-game-win-streak-ends-notre-dame & https://www.biography.com/athlete/john-wooden

68. Jack Ewing, *Faster, Higher, Farther – The Volkswagen Scandal* 66. https://www.nytimes.com/2006/05/21/opinion/21swartz.html

69. Mimi Swartz, *The Three Faces of Ken Lay*, May 21, 2006

70. Alex Kantrowitz, *Always Day One*

71. https://www.thestreet.com/story/10867574/1/the-rise-and- fall-of-blockbuster-the-long-rewinding-road.html

72. https://www.inc.com/minda-zetlin/netflix-blockbuster- meeting-marc-randolph-reed-hastings-john-antioco.html

73. https://stockanalysis.com/stocks/nflx/revenue/

74. https://www.newyorker.com/business/currency/where-nokia-went-wrong

75. Nate Bargatze, *Full Time Magic*

76. https://www.detroitnews.com/story/business/2019/03/13/michigan-born-kmart-uncertain-future/3032679002/

77. https://www.britannica.com/topic/PARC-company

78.https://web.stanford.edu/dept/SUL/sites/mac/parc.html#:~:text=The%20closest%20thing%20in%20the,had%20been%20d eveloped%20at%20PARC.

79. Andy Groves, *Only The Paranoid Survive*

80. Noah Kerner and Gene Pressman, *Chasing Cool*

81. Clayton Christensen, *The Innovator's Dilemma*

82. *Inc. Magazine*, March 2017, p. 90

83. https://www.inc.com/magazine/20040301/closingthedeal.ht ml

84. Malcolm Gladwell, *Tipping Point* 251

85. Ecolaii.wordpress.com

86. Cadbury website / History

87. https://www.cadbury.co.uk/our-story#:~:text=In%201824%2C%20John%20Cadbury%20opened,were%20driven%20by%20his%20beliefs.

88. https://www.referenceforbusiness.com/biography/F- L/Kelleher-Herb-1931.html

89. https://www.linkedin.com/pulse/20130403215758- 22330283-the-importance-of-scheduling-nothing/

90. Adam Grant, *Originals*

91. https://aminoapps.com/c/disney/page/blog/oswald-the-luck- rabbit-and-the-villain-from- up/G5g6_0gwhnuLZ2wVdba73YQzV7Rz4oLwoB7

92. Robert Townsend, *Up the Organization*

93. https://www.cnbc.com/2020/09/22/how-netflix-almost-lost-the-movie-rental-wars-to-blockbuster.html

94. Pat Williams, *Lead like Walt*

95 Phil Knight, *Shoe Dog: A Memoir by the Creator of Nike*

96. https://www.thinkwithgoogle.com/future-of- marketing/creativity/the-curious-case-of-creativity/

97. *Plato*, 1924a

98. https://www.psychologytoday.com/ca/blog/hide-and-seek/201303/plato-poetry?amp

99. Alvin Toffler, *Future Shock*

100. Seth Goldenburg, *Radical Curiosity*

101. https://d23.com/section/walt-disney-archives/walts-quotes/

102. https://techcrunch.com/2012/04/09/instagram-story-facebook-acquisition/

103. Stephen M. R. Covey, *The Speed of Trust*

104. Tony Hsieh, *Delivering Happiness*

105. Gabriel Weinberg and Justin Mares, *Traction*

106. *The Diary Of A CEO: The "Winning Expert": How To Become The Best You Can Be*: Sir David Brailsford l E115

107. James Clear, *Atomic Habits*

108. Dictionary.com

109. https://champions-speakers.co.uk/news/ultimate-guide- marginal-gains#:~:text=Definition%20of%20marginal%20gains%3A%20 The,British%20Cycling%20team's%20recent%20success.

110. "The True Failure Rate of Small Business," Entrepreneur, Jan. 3, 2021,https://www.entrepreneur.com/starting-a-business/the-true-failure-rate-of-small-businesses/361350

111. https://projul.com/blog/8-reasons-why-construction- companies-fail/

112. www.restaurantbusinessonline.com

113. https://blog.hubspot.com/sales/how-to-increase-net-sales- per-salesperson-infographic

114. https://www.visualvisitor.com/the-average-company-spends-10k-15k-hiring-an-individual-and-only-2k-a-year-in-sales- training/

115. https://www.forbes.com/sites/blakemorgan/2019/09/24/50- stats-that-prove-the-value-of-customer- experience/?sh=78f9ad9a4ef2

116. Source: "Understanding Customers," Ruby Newell-Legner

117. Source: White House Office of Consumer Affairs

118. Source: Marketing Metrics

119. Source: Tech Crunch

120. Source: New Voice Media

121. Source: White House Office of Consumer Affairs

122. Source: Harris Interactive

123. Source: White House Office of Consumer Affairs

124. Kristen Smaby, *Being Human is Good Business*

125. Harvey Mackay, *Swim with the Sharks Without Being Eaten Alive*

126. Marc Benioff, *Behind the Cloud*

127. Marc Benioff, *Behind the Cloud*

128. https://academic-accelerator.com/encyclopedia/intelligent-disobedience

129. https://simplypsychology.org/milgram.html

130. Jack Ewing and Joel Richards, *Faster, Higher, Farther: The Volkswagen Scandal*

131. Ray Dalio, *Principles*

132. Stanley Milgram, *Obedience to Authority: An Experimental View*

133. https://www.foodsafetynews.com/2013/02/peanut-corporation-of-america-from-inception-to-indictment-a- timeline/

134. Ryan Holiday, *Courage is Calling*

135. https://winstonchurchill.org/resources/quotes/famous- quotations-and-stories/

136. Google Dictionary

137. Ryan Holiday, *Perennial Sellers*

138. Alex Kantrowitz, *Always Day One*

139. Dictionary.com

140. https://time.com/4922108/hurricane-harvey-matress-mack-houston/

141. https://www.cnbc.com/2017/08/31/houstons-gallery-furniture-turns-stores-into-shelters-to-help-victims.html

142. https://toughmudder.com/

143. https://www.comparably.com/companies/hubspot/mission

144. Al Ries and Jack Trout, *Positioning*

145. Sam Walton, *Made In America*

146. https://jobs.dormanproducts.com/content/Why-Work-At- Dorman/

147. Dictionary.com

148. Grant Cardone, *The 10x Rule*

149. https://grantcardone.com/4th-degree-of-action-massive- action/

150. https://www.freshworks.com/freshsales-crm/resources/grant-cardone-10x-rule-blog/

151. https://www.greenleaf.org/about-us-3/robert-k-greenleaf- biography/

152. Merriam-Webster.com

153. Dictionary.com

154. *Harvard Business Review*, 2017 Nov-Dec, p. 39

155. https://www.adammendler.com/adams-interviews

156. Angela Duckworth, *Grit*

157. Leslie Berlin, *The Man Behind the Microchip*

158. https://www.theguardian.com/world/2006/nov/26/film.usa

159. https://www.pbs.org/wgbh/americanexperience/films/walt-disney/

160. https://www.nytimes.com/2018/03/30/sports/catholic- basketball-final-four.html

161. Dictionary.com

162. https://www.c2ti.com/collaboration-noun-the-action-of-working-with-someone-to-produce-or-create-something/

163. Phil Knight, *Shoe Dog: A Memoir by the Creator of Nike*

164. https://www.entrepreneur.com/growing-a-business/philip-h-knight/197534

165. https://www.statista.com/statistics/217489/revenue-per-employee-of-selected-tech-companies/

166. https://qz.com/924167/ibm-remote-work-pioneer-is-calling-thousands-of-employees-back-to-the-office/, https://hbr.org/2014/10/workspaces-that-move-people

167. Ted Kinni, *Be Our Guest*

168. Tony Hseih, *Delivering Happiness*

169. http://www.leancxscore.com/lean-cx-score-80-of-ceos-believe-they-provide-superior-service-just-8-of-customers- agree/

170. https://hbr.org/2022/11/when-ceos-engage-directly-with- customers

171. Tracy Maylett, E.D. - *The Employee Experience: How to Attract Talent, Retain Top Performers, and Drive Results*

172. https://paddlingmag.com/stories/columns/reflections/expedition-behavior/

173. Daniel Coyle, *The Culture Code*

174. https://www.fastcompany.com/3048503/6-surprising-insights-of-successful-employee-engagement

175. https://www.myrocketcareer.com/about-us/our- philosophies/

176. https://www.myrocketcareer.com/about-us/our- philosophies/

177. https://hbr.org/2013/07/employee-engagement-does-more

178. https://inside.6q.io/benefits-of-engaged-employees/

179. Gallup.com

180. SABA.com

181. https://www.cornerstoneondemand.com/resources/article/william-kahn-qa-founding-father-engagement/

182. https://www.firstarriving.com/engagement-drives- performance/

183. https://learnpatch.com/2018/07/william-kahn-father-of- employee-engagement/

184. https://www.encyclopedia.com/humanities/dictionaries- thesauruses-pictures-and-press-releases/vibe-0

185. https://www.dutchbros.com/our-story

186. Dictionary.com

187. helpscout.net / Gregory Ciotti

188. HobbyLobby.com https://newsroom.hobbylobby.com/corporate-background#:~:text=Offering%20customers%20exceptional%20selection%20and,strengthen%20individuals%20and%20nurture%20families

To all my friends and followers on social media who either gave me that plucky blue thumbs up, red heart, green clap, or a quick kind word in the comments - thank you!

Jeff Guerra - Nathan Starr - Justin Henry - Troy Van Go - Ismael Sanchez - Jeffrey King - Brianna Leonard - John Leonard - Jeriah Steward - Savanna Ragsdale - Jordan Warner - Caleb Colstad - Pete Bryant - Paula Watson - Bryan Harris - Ambur Bell - Mary Nhin - Bobby Greene - Sherryl Weeks - Justin Cranfield - Mark Camp - Fereti Sa'au - David Segovia Vargas - Georgia Crawley – Susan Ross Tiffany - Jerry Skaggs - Michael Crawford - Dena Mossop - Frances Tinsley - Kyle Price - Dunya Elbasan - Dean Miles - Nic Armbruster - Randall Anoatubby - Robert Morris - Becky Rhoades - Michael Carter - Kevin Walkup - Matthew Massie - Sam Allen - Eric Gelly - Allen Ashcraft - Bella Ragsdale - LaRenda Morgan - Dan O'Connor - Sarah Anderson - Dan Pogue - John Winsor - Alex Baird - Jarod Nottingham - Harold Curtis - Carolyn Marks Curtis - Janette Perryman Maxell – Rae Heath - Jay Hall - Dawn Coday - Cheryl Accardi - Kirk Hastings - Adam Ragsdale - Jerrod Murr - Pamela Young - Glenn Cranfield - Bobby Christopher - Brian Mastin - Dustin Garza - Raina Like' - Mike Coday - Joe Baranello - Jay Tindall - Cindy von Hagel - Kristie Tevault - Susan Tafelski-Curtis - Deanna Ragsdale - Derrin & Shayna Bollinger - Savanna Ragsdale - Angela Donadio - Brittany Weiser - Jenni Mailand Godwin - Mark Miller - Edie Guidry Fleck - Dianne Stephenson Burton - Jason Black - Carter Calvert - Diana Colclazier Parker - Pitty Guy Cy Pittman - Tony Serrano - Kyle Price - Camille McCullough - John Havens - Janet Sheppard - Patrick Horning - Lori Jacobs-Tregoning - Shannon Murphy Weis - Inez Freman - Robert Kelley - Parker Hastie – Vanessa Dunn - Riley Bishop - Bob Meyer - Ric Shields - Tiffany Randall Riggs - Vince Smith - Ron Truelove - Ronnie DeChambeau - Dan Coday - Jimmy Thomas - David Vance - Doug Wright - Stephen White - Renae McCooey - Kimberly Phillips - Benny Gagliardi - Aaron Owens - Jennier Dillman - Kevin Worden - Kirk Gurney - Troy Gardner - Tracy Eidson-Zentz - Seth Carper - Glenda Speer - Jessica Buffington - Arlene Baker - Tanna Spotts - Dwight Turner - Candi Turner - Stacey Pruitt - Megan Marek Sanders - Renzo Gianmarco Filomeno -

Andrea Thomas - Dawne Vernon-Erickson - Josh Daugherty - Debra Richardson-Reininger - Jesse Silva - Brian Leonard - Timothy Melvin - Brian Ramey - Eddy Brewer - Chris Loggins - Kristy Kidwell Colley - Lori Boyle - Brad Woody - Gary Shockley - Jamey Dolby - Troy Van Go - Linda Garrison - Jill Borders Allen - Jack Joiner - Lindsey Puckett - Dawn Elliott-Stacey - Dustin Jett - Benjamin Stubbs - David Swift - Marin Godwin-Ragsdale - Derrick Sier - Cheryl McFarland Prewitt - Stefanie Shockley - Justin Peterson - Terry Sparks - Brian Woeppel - Holly Vernon-Miller - Lane Hastie - Talon Wolfe - Jonna Pitts - Michelle Metcalf-Leonard - Breanna Jones - Kristin Kubitschek - Tony Ashworth - Tawnya Stewart - Shannon Thieman - Mike Chittum - Michelle Joiner - Brian Fontenot - Cara Crawley - Brianna & Aven Ault - Phillip Church - Garcia Sonia - Rodney Gamble - Elizabeth Wallis Snyder - Micah Curtis - Lisa Workman-Aynes - Denise Abrahamson - Victoria Jo Weatherbie-Thomas - Melissa Pierce - Hunter Pistole - Carol Godwin - Lynette Harper - Mark Warner - Greg Wiles - Cara Beal - Katherine Porter - JanetLee Amlaner Swink - Pam & Larry Love - Lee Chiroff - Taylor Aldridge - Robb Higdon - Leah Miller - George Lamelza - Kade Uy – Neha Ghelani - Sandee Dummitt - Brandon Wykoff - Mark Delaney - Cheryl Blow - Fred Chilton - Ron Woods - Stephen Aristophanes Martin - Thomas P Donovan - Daniel Godwin - Kolton Lynn - Jeff Jackson